creation and discovery

ESSAYS IN CRITICISM AND AESTHETICS

eliseo vivas

Essay Index Reprint Series

BOOKS FOR LIBRARIES PRESS
FREEPORT, NEW YORK

Library of Congress Cataloging in Publication Data

Vivas, Eliseo.
   Creation and discovery.

   (Essay index reprint series)
   1. Literature--Aesthetics.   2.   Literature--History
and criticism.   3.   Criticism.   I.   Title.
[PN45.V55 1972]   801'.93   72-3365
ISBN 0-8369-2931-4

PREFACE

THIS volume consists of a certain number of Essays and Addresses which have been delivered or written during the last eleven years. None of them have any relation to party politics except perhaps, to a very slight extent, the review of Mr. Morley's *Cobden.* But even in this case it seems to me that the changes that have come over current political theories since Mr. Cobden's death are so great that an estimate of certain particular aspects of his public career may be attempted without unduly raising controversies in which modern politicians are immediately concerned.

There is no bond of connection uniting the various Essays which find a place in this collection into anything of the nature of an organic whole. The second and third, indeed, are so far related that they deal with the life and work of two great men of

the eighteenth century who were almost exactly
contemporaries.   But the Essay on Berkeley is a
biographical study : that on Handel in the main
a critical and æsthetic one.   The fourth and fifth
Essays may both be said, though in different ways, to
touch on the questions which have been, and are
being, raised by the application of economic theories
to political practice.   While the sixth and seventh
differ from the rest in being altogether removed from
the sphere of ordinary practical interest.   Though
they were written at different periods, and for different audiences, they probably gain by being read
together, and in the order in which they appear in
this volume.

My thanks are due to the Editors of the various
journals in which any of these Essays may have
originally appeared for permission to republish
them.

    4 CARLTON GARDENS,
      1st *March* 1893.

CONTENTS

I

THE PLEASURES OF READING[1]

IT has probably not been the lot of many of my predecessors in the distinguished post to which you have elected me, to deliver a Rectorial Address under circumstances more adverse to the deliberate reflection and the careful preparation which such a performance requires. So strongly do I feel the extreme difficulty of saying anything worthy of this place and of this audience at a time when the daily and even hourly calls upon me are incessant, that I should have been disposed to defer to a more convenient season my first public appearance amongst you. From this, however, I was deterred by one dominant consideration; namely, that if the Rectorial installation were deferred till next year, or the year after,

[1] Lord Rector's Address, delivered at St. Andrews University, 10th December 1887.

I should have no opportunity of meeting those who interested themselves in the last Rectorial election. In University life, generation succeeds generation with such rapidity, that the leaders among the students of one year are the departed heroes of the next. And I prefer, therefore, even under the somewhat adverse circumstances which I have indicated, to meet those who took a principal part in the contest of last November, whether for or against me, to all the advantages which my audience might be expected to derive from a postponement of my Address.

I will confess to you at the outset that I have been much embarrassed in the selection of a subject. Not a few of my predecessors have found themselves, I should imagine, in a similar difficulty. A Rectorial Address might, so I was informed, be about anything. But this " anything " is too apt upon further investigation to resolve itself into "nothing." Some topics are too dull. Some are too controversial. Some interest only the few. Some are too great a strain upon the speaker who has to prepare them. Some too severely tax the patience of the audience which has to listen to them. And I confess to have been much perplexed in my search for a topic on which I could say something to which you would have patience to listen, or on which I might find it profitable to speak.

One theme, however, there is, not inappropriate to the place in which I stand, nor, I hope, unwelcome to the audience which I address. The youngest of you have left behind that period of youth during which it seems inconceivable that any book should afford recreation except a story-book. Many of you are just reaching the period when, at the end of your prescribed curriculum, the whole field and compass of literature lies outspread before you ; when, with faculties trained and disciplined, and the edge of curiosity not dulled or worn with use, you may enter at your leisure into the intellectual heritage of the centuries.

Now the question of how to read and what to read has of late filled much space in the Daily Papers, if it cannot strictly speaking be said to have profoundly occupied the public mind. But you need be under no alarm. I am not going to supply you with a new list of the hundred books most worth reading, nor am I about to take the world into my confidence in respect of my "favourite passages from the best

authors." Nor again do I address myself to the professed student, to the fortunate individual with whom
literature or science is the business as well as the
pleasure of life. I have not the qualifications which
would enable me to undertake such a task with the
smallest hope of success. My theme is humble though
the audience to whom I desire to speak is large; for
I speak to the ordinary reader with ordinary capacities
and ordinary leisure, to whom reading is, or ought
to be, not a business but a pleasure; and my theme
is the enjoyment, not, mark you, the improvement,
nor the glory, nor the profit, but the *enjoyment*, which
may be derived by such an one from books.

It is perhaps due to the controversial habits
engendered by my unfortunate profession, that I find
no easier method of making my own view clear than
that of contrasting with it what I regard as an erroneous view held by somebody else : and in the present
case the doctrine which I shall choose as a foil to my
own, is one which has been stated with the utmost
force and directness by that brilliant and distinguished writer, Mr. Frederic Harrison.[1] He has,
as many of you know, recently given us in a series

[1] Cf. *The Choice of Books.*

of excellent essays his opinion on the principles which should guide us in the choice of books. Against that part of his treatise which is occupied with specific recommendations of certain authors I have not a word to say. He has resisted all the temptations to eccentricity which so easily beset the modern critic. Every book which he praises deserves his praise, and has long been praised by the world at large. I do not, indeed, hold that the verdict of the world is necessarily binding on the individual conscience. I admit to the full that there is an enormous quantity of hollow devotion, of withered orthodoxy divorced from living faith, in the eternal chorus of praise which goes up from every literary altar to the memory of the immortal dead. Nevertheless, every critic is bound to recognise, as Mr. Harrison recognises, that he must put down to individual peculiarity any difference he may have with the general verdict of the ages ; he must feel that mankind are not likely to be in a conspiracy of error as to the kind of literary work which conveys to them the highest literary enjoyment, and that in such cases at least *securus judicat orbis terrarum.*

But it is quite possible to hold that any work

recommended by Mr. Harrison is worth repeated reading, and yet to reject utterly the theory of study by which these recommendations are prefaced. For Mr. Harrison is a ruthless censor. His *index expurgatorius* includes, so far as I can discover, the whole catalogue of the British Museum, with the exception of a small remnant which might easily be contained in about thirty or forty volumes. The vast remainder he contemplates with feelings apparently not merely of indifference but of active aversion. He surveys the boundless and ever-increasing waste of books with emotions compounded of disgust and dismay. He is almost tempted to say in his haste that the invention of printing has been an evil one for humanity. In the habits of miscellaneous reading, born of a too easy access to libraries, circulating and other, he sees many soul-destroying tendencies; and his ideal reader would appear to be a gentleman who rejects with a lofty scorn all in history that does not pass for being first rate in importance, and all in literature that is not admitted to be first rate in quality.

Now I am far from denying that this theory is plausible. Of all that has been written it is certain that the professed student can master but an infinitesimal fraction. Of that fraction the ordinary reader can master but a very small part. What advice then can be better than to select for study the few masterpieces that have come down to us, and to treat as non-existent the huge but undistinguished remainder? We are like travellers passing hastily through some ancient city filled with memorials of many generations and more than one great civilisation. Our time is short. Of what may be seen we can only see at best but a trifling fragment. Let us then take care that we waste none of our precious moments upon that which is less than the most excellent. So preaches Mr. Frederic Harrison : and when a doctrine which put thus may seem not only wise but obvious, is further supported by such assertions as that habits of miscellaneous reading "close the mind to what is spiritually sustaining" by "stuffing it with what is simply curious," or that such methods of study are worse than no habits of study at all because they "gorge and enfeeble" the mind by "excess in that which cannot nourish," I almost feel that in venturing to dissent from it I may be attacking not merely the teaching of common sense but the inspirations of a high morality.

Yet I am convinced that, for most persons, the views thus laid down by Mr. Harrison are wrong, and that what he describes, with characteristic vigour, as "an impotent voracity for desultory information" is in reality a most desirable, and a not too common form, of mental appetite. I have no sympathy whatever with the horror he expresses at the "incessant accumulation of fresh books." I am never tempted to regret that Gutenberg was born into the world. I care not at all though the "cataract of printed stuff," as Mr. Harrison calls it, should flow and still flow on until the catalogues of our libraries should make libraries themselves. I am prepared indeed, to express sympathy almost amounting to approbation for any one who would check all writing which was *not* intended for the printer. I pay no tribute of grateful admiration to those who have oppressed mankind with the dubious blessing of the penny post. But the ground of the distinction is plain. We are always obliged to read our letters, and are sometimes obliged to answer them. But who obliges us to wade through the piled-up lumber of an ancient library, or to skim more than we like off the frothy foolishness poured forth in ceaseless streams by our circulating libraries?

Dead dunces do not importune us; Grub Street does
not ask for a reply by return of post. Even their
living successors need hurt no one who possesses the
very moderate degree of social courage required to
make the admission that he has not read the last new
novel or the current number of a fashionable magazine.

But this is not the view of Mr. Harrison. To him
the position of any one having free access to a large
library is fraught with issues so tremendous that, in
order adequately to describe it, he has to seek for
parallels in two of the most highly-wrought episodes
in fiction—the Ancient Mariner, becalmed and thirst-
ing on the tropic ocean: Bunyan's Christian in the
crisis of spiritual conflict. But there is here, surely,
some error and some exaggeration. Has miscellaneous reading all the dreadful consequences which
Mr. Harrison depicts? Has it any of them? His
declarations about the intellect being "gorged and
enfeebled" by the absorption of too much information, expresses no doubt with great vigour an analogy,
for which there is high authority, between the human
mind and the human stomach; but surely it is an
analogy which may be pressed too far. I have often
heard of the individual whose excellent natural gifts

have been so overloaded with huge masses of undigested and indigestible learning that they have had no chance of healthy development. But though I have often heard of this personage, I have never met him, and I believe him to be mythical. It is true, no doubt, that many learned people are dull: but there is no indication whatever that they are dull because they are learned. True dulness is seldom acquired; it is a natural grace, the manifestations of which, however modified by education, remain in substance the same. Fill a dull man to the brim with knowledge, and he will not become less dull, as the enthusiasts for education vainly imagine; but neither will he become duller, as Mr. Harrison appears to suppose. He will remain in essence what he always has been and always must have been. But whereas his dulness would, if left to itself, have been merely vacuous, it may have become, under careful cultivation, pretentious and pedantic.

I would further point out to you that, while there is no ground in experience for supposing that a keen interest in those facts which Mr. Harrison describes as "merely curious," has any stupefying effect upon the mind, or has any tendency to render it insensible to the higher things of literature and art, there is positive evidence that many of those who have most deeply felt the charm of these higher things have been consumed by that omnivorous appetite for knowledge which excites Mr. Harrison's especial indignation. Dr. Johnson, for instance, though deaf to some of the most delicate harmonies of verse, was, without question, a very great critic. Yet, in Dr. Johnson's opinion, literary history, which is for the most part composed of facts which Mr. Harrison would regard as insignificant, about authors whom he would regard as pernicious, was the most delightful of studies. Again, consider the case of Lord Macaulay. Lord Macaulay did everything Mr. Harrison says he ought not to have done. From youth to age he was continuously occupied in "gorging and enfeebling" his intellect, by the unlimited consumption of every species of literature, from the masterpieces of the age of Pericles, to the latest rubbish from the circulating library. It is not told of him that his intellect suffered by the process; and, though it will hardly be claimed for him that he was a great critic, none will deny that he possessed the keenest susceptibilities for literary excellence in many languages and in every form. If Englishmen and Scotchmen do not satisfy you, I will take a Frenchman. The most accomplished critic whom France has produced is, by general admission, St. Beuve. His capacity for appreciating supreme perfection in literature will be disputed by none ; yet the great bulk of his vast literary industry was expended upon the lives and writings of authors whose lives Mr. Harrison would desire us to forget, and whose writings almost wring from him the wish that the art of printing had never been discovered.

I am even bold enough to hazard the conjecture (I trust he will forgive me) that Mr. Harrison's life may be quoted against Mr. Harrison's theory. I entirely decline to believe without further evidence that the writings whose vigour of style and of thought have been the delight of us all, are the product of his own system. I hope I do him no wrong, but I cannot help thinking that, if we knew the truth, we should find that he followed the practice of those worthy physicians who, after prescribing the most abstemious diet to their patients, may be seen partaking freely and, to all appearances, safely of the most succulent and the most unwholesome of the forbidden dishes.

It has to be noted that Mr. Harrison's list of the books which deserve perusal would seem to indicate that, in his opinion, the pleasures to be derived from literature are chiefly pleasures of the imagination. Poets, dramatists, and novelists form the chief portion of the somewhat meagre fare which is specifically permitted to his disciples.   Now, though I have already stated that the list is not one of which any person is likely to assert that it contains books which ought to be excluded, yet, even from the point of view of what may be termed æsthetic enjoyment, the field in which we are allowed to take our pleasures seems to me unduly restricted.

Contemporary poetry, for instance, on which Mr. Harrison bestows a good deal of hard language, has, and must have, for the generation which produces it certain qualities not likely to be possessed by any other.   Charles Lamb has somewhere declared that a pun loses all its virtue as soon as the momentary quality of the intellectual and social atmosphere in which it was born has changed its character.   What is true of this, the humblest effort of verbal art, is

true, in a different measure and degree, of all, even
of the highest, forms of literature.   To some extent
every work requires interpretation to generations
who are separated by differences of thought or
education from the age in which it was originally
produced.   That this is so with every book which
depends for its interest upon feelings and fashions
which have utterly vanished, no one will be disposed,
I imagine, to deny.   Butler's *Hudibras*, for instance,
which was the delight of a gay and witty society, is to
me, at least, not unfrequently dull.   Of some works,
no doubt, which made a noise in their day it seems
impossible to detect the slightest trace of charm.
But this is not the case with *Hudibras*.   Its merits
are obvious.   That they should have appealed to a
generation sick of the reign of the " Saints " is precisely what we should have expected.   But to us,
who are not sick of the reign of the Saints, they
appeal but imperfectly.   The attempt to reproduce
artificially the frame of mind of those who first read
the poem is not only an effort, but is to most people,
at all events, an unsuccessful effort.   What is true of
Hudibras is true also, though in an inconceivably
smaller degree, of those great works of imagination

which deal with the elemental facts of human character and human passion. Yet even on these, time does, though lightly, lay his hand. Wherever what may be called " historic sympathy " is required there will be some diminution of the enjoyment which those must have felt who were the poet's contemporaries. We look, so to speak, at the same splendid landscape as they, but distance has made it necessary for us to aid our natural vision with glasses, and some loss of light will thus inevitably be produced, and some inconvenience from the difficulty of truly adjusting the focus. Of all authors, Homer would, I suppose, be thought to suffer least from such drawbacks. But yet in order to listen to Homer's accents with the ears of an ancient Greek, we must be able, among other things, to enter into a view about the gods which is as far removed from what we should describe as religious sentiment as it is from the frigid ingenuity of those later poets who regarded the deities of Greek mythology as so many wheels in the supernatural machinery with which it pleased them to carry on the action of their pieces. If we are to accept Mr. Herbert Spencer's views as to the progress of our species, changes of sentiment are likely to occur which will even more seriously interfere with the world's delight in the Homeric poems. When human beings become so nicely "adjusted to their environment," that courage and dexterity in battle will have become as useless among civic virtues as an old helmet is among weapons of war ; when fighting gets to be looked upon with the sort of disgust excited in us by cannibalism ; and when public opinion shall regard a warrior much in the same light that we regard a hangman, I do not see how any fragment of that vast and splendid literature which depends for its interest upon deeds of heroism and the joy of battle, is to retain its ancient charm. About these remote contingencies, however, I am glad to think that neither you nor I need trouble our heads ; and if I parenthetically allude to them now, it is merely as an illustration of a truth not always sufficiently remembered, and as an excuse for those who find in the genuine, though possibly second-rate, productions of their own age a charm for which they search in vain among the mighty monuments of the past.

But I leave this train of thought, which has perhaps already taken me too far, in order to point out a more fundamental error, as I think it, which

arises from regarding literature solely from this high
æsthetic standpoint. The pleasures of imagination
derived from the best literary models, form without
doubt the most exquisite portion of the enjoyment
which we may extract from books; but they do not
in my opinion form the largest portion if we take
into account mass as well as quality in our calculation.
There is the literature which appeals to the imagination or the fancy, some stray specimens of which Mr.
Harrison will permit us to peruse; but is there not
also the literature which satisfies the curiosity? Is
this vast storehouse of pleasure to be thrown hastily
aside because many of the facts which it contains
are alleged to be insignificant, because the appetite to
which they minister is said to be morbid? Consider a
little. We are here dealing with one of the strongest
intellectual impulses of rational beings. Animals,
as a rule, trouble themselves but little about anything
unless they want either to eat it or to run away from
it. Interest in, and wonder at, the works of nature
and the doings of man are products of civilisation,
and excite emotions which do not diminish, but increase with increasing knowledge and cultivation.
Feed them and they grow; minister to them and

C

they will greatly multiply. We hear much indeed of what is called "idle curiosity," but I am loth to brand any form of curiosity as necessarily idle. Take, for example, one of the most singular, but, in this age, one of the most universal, forms in which it is accustomed to manifest itself : I mean that of an exhaustive study of the contents of the morning and evening papers. It is certainly remarkable that any person who has nothing to get by it should destroy his eyesight and confuse his brain by a conscientious attempt to master the dull and doubtful details of the European diary daily transmitted to us by "Our Special Correspondent." But it must be remembered that this is only a somewhat unprofitable exercise of that disinterested love of knowledge which moves men to penetrate the Polar snows, to build up systems of philosophy, or to explore the secrets of the remotest heavens. It has in it the rudiments of infinite and varied delights. It *can* be turned, and it *should* be turned, into a curiosity for which nothing that has been done, or thought, or suffered, or believed, no law which governs the world of matter or the world of mind, can be wholly alien or uninteresting.

Truly it is a subject for astonishment that, instead

of expanding to the utmost the employment of this
pleasure-giving faculty, so many persons should set
themselves to work to limit its exercise by all kinds
of arbitrary regulations. Some there are, for example,
who tell us that the acquisition of knowledge is all very
well, but that it must be *useful* knowledge, meaning
usually thereby that it must enable a man to get on
in a profession, pass an examination, shine in conversation, or obtain a reputation for learning. But even
if they mean something higher than this, even if they
mean that knowledge to be worth anything must
subserve ultimately if not immediately the material
or spiritual interests of mankind, the doctrine is one
which should be energetically repudiated. I admit,
of course, at once, that discoveries the most apparently
remote from human concerns have often proved themselves of the utmost commercial or manufacturing
value. But they require no such justification for
their existence, nor were they striven for with any
such object. Navigation is not the final cause of
astronomy, nor telegraphy of electro-dynamics, nor
dye-works of chemistry. And if it be true that the
desire of knowledge for the sake of knowledge was
the animating motive of the great men who first

wrested her secrets from nature, why should it not also be enough for us, to whom it is not given to discover, but only to learn as best we may what has been discovered by others?

Another maxim, more plausible but equally pernicious, is that superficial knowledge is worse than no knowledge at all. That "a little knowledge is a dangerous thing" is a saying which has now got currency as a proverb stamped in the mint of Pope's versification; of Pope, who with the most imperfect knowledge of Greek translated Homer, with the most imperfect knowledge of the Elizabethan drama edited Shakespeare, and with the most imperfect knowledge of philosophy wrote the Essay on Man. But what is this "little knowledge" which is supposed to be so dangerous? What is it "little" in relation to? If in relation to what there is to know, then all human knowledge is little. If in relation to what actually is known by somebody, then we must condemn as "dangerous" the knowledge which Archimedes possessed of Mechanics, or Copernicus of Astronomy; for a shilling primer and a few weeks' study will enable any student to outstrip in mere information some of the greatest teachers of the past. No doubt, that little knowledge which thinks itself to be great, may possibly be a dangerous, as it certainly is a most ridiculous, thing. We have all suffered under that eminently absurd individual who on the strength of one or two volumes, imperfectly apprehended by himself, and long discredited in the estimation of every one else, is prepared to supply you on the shortest notice with a dogmatic solution of every problem suggested by this "unintelligible world"; or the political variety of the same pernicious genus, whose statecraft consists in the ready application to the most complex question of national interest of some high-sounding commonplace which has done weary duty on a thousand platforms, and which even in its palmiest days was never fit for anything better than a peroration. But in our dislike of the individual do not let us mistake the diagnosis of his disease. He suffers not from ignorance but from stupidity. Give him learning and you make him not wise, but only more pretentious in his folly.

I say then that so far from a little knowledge being undesirable, a little knowledge is all that on most subjects any of us can hope to attain, and that, as a source not of worldly profit but of personal

pleasure, it may be of incalculable value to its possessor.　But it will naturally be asked, " How are we
to select from among the infinite number of things
which may be known those which it is best worth
while for us to know?"　We are constantly being
told to concern ourselves with learning what is important, and not to waste our energies upon what is
insignificant.　But what are the marks by which we
shall recognise the important, and how is it to be
distinguished from the insignificant?　A precise and
complete answer to this question which shall be true
for all men cannot be given.　I am considering
knowledge, recollect, as it ministers to enjoyment,
and from this point of view each unit of information
is obviously of importance in proportion as it increases the general sum of enjoyment which we
obtain, or expect to obtain, from knowledge.　This,
of course, makes it impossible to lay down precise
rules which shall be an equally sure guide to all sorts
and conditions of men ; for in this, as in other matters,
tastes must differ, and against real difference of taste
there is no appeal.

There is, however, one caution which it may be
worth your while to keep in view,—Do not be per-

suaded into applying any general proposition on this subject with a foolish impartiality to every kind of knowledge. There are those who tell you that it is the broad generalities and the far-reaching principles which govern the world, which are alone worthy of your attention. A fact which is not an illustration of a law in the opinion of these persons appears to lose all its value. Incidents which do not fit into some great generalisation; events which are merely picturesque; details which are merely curious—they dismiss as unworthy the interest of a reasoning being. Now even in science this doctrine in its extreme form does not hold good. The most scientific of men have taken profound interest in the investigation of facts from the determination of which they do not anticipate any material addition to our knowledge of the laws which regulate the Universe. In these matters, I need hardly say that I speak wholly without authority. But I have always been under the impression that an investigation which has cost hundreds of thousands of pounds; which has stirred on three occasions the whole scientific community throughout the civilised world; on which has been expended the utmost skill in the construction of

instruments and their application to purposes of
research (I refer to the attempts made to determine
the distance of the sun by observations of the transit
of Venus) would, even if they had been brought to a
successful issue, have furnished mankind with the
knowledge of no new astronomical principle.[1] The
laws which govern the motions of the solar system,
the proportions which the various elements in that
system bear to one another, have long been known.
The distance of the sun itself is known within limits
of error relatively speaking not very considerable.
Were the measuring rod we apply to the heavens
based on an estimate of the sun's distance from the
earth, which was wrong by (say) 3 per cent, it
would not to the lay mind seem to affect very
materially our view either of the distribution of the
heavenly bodies or of their motions. And yet this
information, this piece of celestial gossip, would seem
to have been the chief astronomical result expected
from the successful prosecution of an investigation

[1] The accurate determination of the velocity of light would
doubtless be of the greatest importance in Physics. But as regards
astronomical research, in reference to which the Transit of Venus
has been principally observed, the illustration in the text seems
accurate. The amount of possible error is much less than 3
per cent.

in which whole nations have interested themselves.

But though no one can, I think, pretend that
science does not concern itself, and properly concern
itself, with facts which are not to all appearance
illustrations of law, it is undoubtedly true that for
those who desire to extract the greatest pleasure
from science, a knowledge, however elementary, of
the leading principles of investigation and the larger
laws of nature, is the acquisition most to be desired.
To him who is not a specialist, a comprehension of
the broad outlines of the universe as it presents itself
to the scientific imagination is the thing most worth
striving to attain. But when we turn from science
to what is rather vaguely called history, the same
principles of study do not, I think, altogether apply,
and mainly for this reason ;—that while the recognition of the reign of law is the chief amongst the
pleasures imparted by Science, our inevitable ignorance
makes it the least among the pleasures imparted by
History.

It is no doubt true that we are surrounded by
advisers who tell us that all study of the past is
barren except in so far as it enables us to determine

the principles by which the evolution of human
societies is governed.   How far such an investigation
has been up to the present time fruitful in results it
would be unkind to inquire.   That it will ever enable
us to trace with accuracy the course which states and
nations are destined to pursue in the future, or to
account in detail for their history in the past, I do not
in the least believe.   We are borne along like travellers
on some unexplored stream.   We may know enough of
the general configuration of the globe to be sure that
we are making our way towards the ocean.   We may
know enough, by experience or theory, of the laws
regulating the flow of liquids, to conjecture how the
river will behave under the varying influences to
which it may be subject.   More than this we cannot
know.   It will depend largely upon causes which, in
relation to any laws which we are ever likely to discover may properly be called accidental, whether we
are destined sluggishly to drift among fever-stricken
swamps, to hurry down perilous rapids, or to glide
gently through fair scenes of peaceful cultivation.

But leaving on one side ambitious sociological
speculations, and even those more modest but hitherto
more successful investigations into the causes which

have in particular cases been principally operative in producing great political changes, there are still two modes in which we can derive what I may call " spectacular " enjoyment from the study of history. There is first the pleasure which arises from the contemplation of some great historic drama, or some broad and well-marked phase of social development. The story of the rise, greatness, and decay of a nation is like some vast epic which contains as subsidiary episodes the varied stories of the rise, greatness, and decay of creeds, of parties and of statesmen. The imagination is moved by the slow unrolling of this great picture of human mutability, as it is moved by the contrasted permanence of the abiding stars. The ceaseless conflict, the strange echoes of long-forgotten controversies, the confusion of purpose, the successes in which lay deep the seeds of future evils, the failures that ultimately divert the otherwise inevitable danger, the heroism which struggles to the last for a cause foredoomed to defeat, the wickedness which sides with right, and the wisdom which huzzas at the triumph of folly—fate, meanwhile, amidst this turmoil and perplexity, working silently towards the predestined end—all these form together a subject the contemplation of which need surely never weary.

But there is yet another and very different species of enjoyment to be derived from the records of the past, which requires a somewhat different method of study in order that it may be fully tasted. Instead of contemplating as it were from a distance the larger aspects of the human drama, we may elect to move in familiar fellowship amid the scenes and actors of special periods. We may add to the interest we derive from the contemplation of contemporary politics, a similar interest derived from a not less minute, and probably more accurate, knowledge of some comparatively brief passage in the political history of the past. We may extend the social circle in which we move, a circle perhaps narrowed and restricted through circumstances beyond our control, by making intimate acquaintances, perhaps even close friends, among a society long departed, but which, when we have once learnt the trick of it, we may, if it so pleases us, revive.

It is this kind of historical reading which is usually branded as frivolous and useless, and persons who indulge in it often delude themselves into

thinking that the real motive of their investigation
into bygone scenes and ancient scandals, is philosophic
interest in an important historical episode, whereas
in truth it is not the Philosophy which glorifies the
details, but the details which make tolerable the
Philosophy. Consider, for example, the case of the
French Revolution. The period from the taking of
the Bastille to the fall of Robespierre is about the
same as that which very commonly intervenes between
two of our general elections. On these comparatively
few months, libraries have been written. The incidents of every week are matters of familiar knowledge.
The character and the biography of every actor in the
drama has been made the subject of minute study ;
and by common admission there is no more fascinating
page in the history of the world. But the interest is
not what is commonly called philosophic, it is
personal. Because the Revolution is the dominant
fact in Modern History, therefore people suppose
that the doings of this or that provincial lawyer,
tossed into temporary eminence and eternal infamy
by some freak of the revolutionary wave, or the
atrocities committed by this or that mob, half drunk
with blood, rhetoric, and alcohol, are of transcendent

importance. In truth their interest is great, but
their importance is small. What we are concerned to
know as students of the philosophy of History is, not
the character of each turn and eddy in the great
social cataract, but the manner in which the currents
of the upper stream drew surely in towards the final
plunge, and slowly collected themselves after the
catastrophe again to pursue, at a different level, their
renewed and comparatively tranquil course.

Now, if so much of the interest of the French
Revolution depends upon our minute knowledge of
each passing incident, how much more necessary is
such knowledge when we are dealing with the quiet
nooks and corners of history ; when we are seeking
an introduction, let us say, into the literary society
of Johnson, or the fashionable society of Walpole.
Society, dead or alive, can have no charm without
intimacy, and no intimacy without interest in trifles
which I fear Mr. Harrison would describe as "merely
curious." If we would feel at our ease in any company,
if we wish to find humour in its jokes, and point in its
repartees, we must know something of the beliefs and
the prejudices of its various members, their loves and
their hates, their hopes and their fears, their maladies,

their marriages, and their flirtations.   If these things are beneath our notice, we shall not be the less qualified to serve our queen and country, but need make no attempt to extract pleasure from one of the most delightful departments of literature.

That there is such a thing as trifling information I do not of course question ; but the frame of mind in which the reader is constantly weighing the exact importance to the universe at large of each circumstance which the author presents to his notice is not one conducive to the true enjoyment of a picture whose effect depends upon a multitude of slight and seemingly insignificant touches, which impress the mind often without remaining in the memory.   The best method of guarding against the danger of reading what is useless is to read only what is interesting.   A truth which will seem a paradox to a whole class of readers, fitting objects of our commiseration, who may be often recognised by their habit of asking some adviser for a list of books, and then marking out a scheme of study in the course of which all are to be conscientiously perused.   These unfortunate persons apparently read a book, principally with the object of getting to the end of it. They reach the word " *Finis* " with the same sensation of triumph as an Indian feels who strings a fresh scalp to his girdle. They are not happy unless they mark by some definite performance each step in the weary path of self-improvement.   To begin a volume and not to finish it would be to deprive themselves of this satisfaction ; it would be to lose all the reward of their earlier self-denial by a lapse from virtue at the end.   To skip, according to their literary code, is a species of cheating ; it is a mode of obtaining credit for erudition on false pretences ; a plan by which the advantages of learning are surreptitiously obtained by those who have not won them by honest toil.   But all this is quite wrong.   In matters literary, works have no saving efficacy.   He has only half learnt the art of reading who has not added to it the even more refined accomplishments of skipping and of skimming ; and the first step has hardly been taken in the direction of making literature a pleasure until interest in the subject, and not a desire to spare (so to speak) the author's feelings, or to accomplish an appointed task, is the prevailing motive of the reader.

I have now reached, not indeed the end of my subject, which I have scarcely begun, but the limits inexorably set by the circumstances under which it is treated.   Yet I am unwilling to conclude without meeting an objection to my method of dealing with it, which has I am sure been present to the minds of not a few who have been good enough to listen to me with patience.   It will be said that I have ignored the higher functions of literature, that I have degraded it from its rightful place, by discussing only certain ways in which it may minister to the entertainment of an idle hour : leaving wholly out of sight its contributions to what Mr. Harrison calls our "spiritual sustenance."   Now this is partly because the first of these topics and not the second was the avowed subject of my address ; but it is partly because I am deliberately of opinion that it is the pleasures and not the profits, spiritual or temporal, of literature which most require to be preached in the ear of the ordinary reader.   I hold, indeed, the faith that all such pleasures minister to the development of much that is best in man—mental and moral ; but the charm is broken and the object lost if the remote consequence is consciously pursued to the exclusion of the immediate end.   It will not, I suppose, be denied that the beauties of nature are at least as

well qualified to minister to our higher needs as are
the beauties of literature.   Yet we do not say we
are going to walk to the top of such and such a hill
in order to drink in " spiritual sustenance."   We say
we are going to look at the view.   And I am convinced that this, which is the natural and simple way
of considering literature as well as nature, is also the
true way.   The habit of always requiring some reward for knowledge beyond the knowledge itself, be
that reward some material prize or be it what is
vaguely called self-improvement, is one with which I
confess I have little sympathy, fostered though it is
by the whole scheme of our modern education.   Do
not suppose that I desire the impossible.   I would
not if I could destroy the examination system.   But
there are times, I confess, when I feel tempted somewhat to vary the prayer of the poet, and to ask
whether Heaven has not reserved in pity to this
much educating generation some peaceful desert of
literature as yet unclaimed by the crammer or the
coach ; where it might be possible for the student to
wander, even perhaps to stray, at his own pleasure ;
without finding every beauty labelled, every difficulty
engineered, every nook surveyed, and a professional

cicerone standing at every corner to guide each succeeding traveller along the same well-worn round. If such a wish were granted I would further ask that the domain of knowledge thus "neutralised" should be the literature of our own country. I grant to the full that the systematic study of *some* literature must be a principal element in the education of youth. But why should that literature be our own? Why should we brush off the bloom and freshness from the works to which Englishmen and Scotchmen most naturally turn for refreshment, namely, those written in their own language? Why should we associate them with the memory of hours spent in weary study; in the effort to remember for purposes of examination what no human being would wish to remember for any other; in the struggle to learn something, not because the learner desires to know it, because he desires some one else to know that he knows it? This is the dark side of the examination system—a system necessary and therefore excellent, but one which does, through the very efficiency and thoroughness of the drill by which it imparts knowledge, to some extent impair the most delicate pleasures by which the acquisition of knowledge should be attended.

How great those pleasures may be I trust there are many here who can testify. When I compare the position of the reader of to-day with that of his predecessor of the sixteenth century, I am amazed at the ingratitude of those who are tempted even for a moment to regret the invention of printing and the multiplication of books. There is now no mood of mind to which a man may not administer the appropriate nutriment or medicine at the cost of reaching down a volume from his bookshelf. In every department of knowledge infinitely more is known, and what is known is incomparably more accessible than it was to our ancestors. The lighter forms of literature, good, bad, and indifferent, which have added so vastly to the happiness of mankind, have increased beyond powers of computation, nor do I believe that there is any reason to think that they have elbowed out their more serious and important brethren. It is perfectly possible for a man, not a professed student, and who only gives to reading the leisure hours of a business life, to acquire such a general knowledge of the laws of nature and the facts of history that every great advance made in either department shall be to him both intelligible and interesting; and he may besides have among his familiar friends many a departed worthy whose memory is embalmed in the pages of memoir or biography. All this is ours for the asking. All this we shall ask for if only it be our happy fortune to love for its own sake the beauty and the knowledge to be gathered from books. And if this be our fortune, the world may be kind or unkind, it may seem to us to be hastening on the wings of enlightenment and progress to an imminent millennium, or it may weigh us down with the sense of insoluble difficulty and irremediable wrong; but whatever else it be, so long as we have good health and a good library, it can hardly be dull.

II

BISHOP BERKELEY'S LIFE AND LETTERS[1]

I

BERKELEY'S chief title to fame must always rest on his philosophy. It is as a descendant in the true line of succession from Locke to the modern schools of thought, which are either a development of Locke's principles or a reaction against that development, that he is, and that he deserves to be, chiefly remembered. Yet his life and character had for his contemporaries, and may have for us, an interest quite apart from the details of metaphysical discussion. We may look at him, as they looked at him, not principally as the successor of Locke and the predecessor of Hume, as the almost impersonal author of a subtle philosophical theory, but as the worthy associate of the men who rendered the first fifty years of the eighteenth century

[1] *National Review*, March and April 1883.

illustrious in English literature, as an Irish patriot, as an American philanthropist, as a religious controversialist, as a man of delightful character and converse, simple, devoted, and unworldly. Though it be true, therefore, that—philosophy apart—Berkeley effected little; though he did not write enough to rank in the first class among men of letters, nor perform enough to be counted a successful man of action; though he was neither a great social power, nor a great missionary, nor a great ecclesiastic, it is also true that scarce any man of his generation touched contemporary life at so many points. In reading his not very voluminous works we find ourselves not only in the thick of every great controversy—theological, mathematical, and philosophical—which raged in England during the first half of the eighteenth century, but we get glimpses of life in the most diverse conditions : in the seclusion of Trinity College, Dublin, in the best literary and fashionable society in London, among the prosperous colonists of Rhode Island, among the very far from prosperous peasants and squireens of Cork. And all this in the company of a man endowed with the subtlest of intellects, lit up with a humour the most delicate and urbane.

It is not creditable to the piety with which we cherish the memory of our literary ancestors, that no serious effort should have been made till 120 years after Berkeley's death to collect his scattered writings, and to place on record all that can be discovered of his life. But we may perhaps console ourselves for the fact that some valuable material has thus been lost beyond recall, by reflecting that the work, though begun too late, has at last been admirably carried out. Professor Fraser, in his recent edition of Berkeley's collected works, has not only provided the philosophic student with all the assistance he can possibly require, but (which is more to my present purpose) has enriched it with a most excellent life of his author. Our obligations to him, however, do not end there. Since the publication of the life and letters, some new biographical details of much interest have come to light. Professor Fraser has taken the opportunity, afforded him by the issue of the series of "Philosophic Classics," to insert them in the volume devoted to Berkeley, and has thereby earned a new title to the gratitude of Berkeley's admirers. In this little work Professor Fraser has, with remarkable skill, woven into an organic whole much of the material he formerly divided (in the complete edition) between the works and the life : so that the reader may now obtain an adequate account of the opinions of the philosopher, illustrated by the circumstances under which those opinions were formed and given to the world. This is, without doubt, the proper way to obtain a true view of the life and writings of any author, and not least of Berkeley. But it unfortunately presupposes a wider knowledge of philosophical subjects than most readers possess or care to acquire : and I may, therefore, be doing a service if, by a free use of the materials which Professor Fraser has supplied, I can succeed, without lapsing into metaphysics, in giving an interesting portrait of one of the most interesting figures in our literary history.

For few purposes but those of the almanack-maker does the period we call the "eighteenth century" begin with the year 1701. The precise limits of it can, indeed, be hardly determined; and the terms which we fix for it must not only be to some extent arbitrary, but must vary according to the point of view from which we happen to be considering it. Yet, we may say roughly, that for the purposes respectively of science, philosophy, and theology, it

began (in England at least) with Newton's *Principia*,
published in 1687 ; Locke's *Essay*, published in 1690 ;
and (let not the reader be shocked at the descent)
Toland's deistical work, *Christianity not Mysterious*,
published in 1696.   Trinity College, Dublin, then
just beginning to recover from the civil wars which
in Ireland accompanied the Revolution, was profoundly affected by all three works.   With a readiness to accept new doctrine which has not always
been shown by academic societies, the *Principia* and
the *Essay* became at once part of the studies of the
place, and though I do not know whether the
ponderous " Logics " of Burgersdicius and Smiglecius,
on which it is alleged that Swift's university career
so nearly made shipwreck a few years before,[1] were
discarded from the " curriculum," there can be no
doubt that the whole current of opinion ran violently
against scholastic methods, and in favour of Newton's
physics and Locke's philosophy.   As for Toland, the
effect of his work in Dublin was more violent and, for
our present purpose, nearly as important.   *Christianity
not Mysterious* was burnt by the common hangman,
censured by the Irish Parliament, denounced from

[1] Swift took his degree in 1685, the year of Berkeley's birth.

every pulpit in the city, whilst its author, much delighted at the turmoil he had raised, found it expedient to leave the country. " A sermon against his errors was as much expected," says Mr. Hunt,[1] "as if it had been prescribed in the rubric : and an Irish peer gave it as a reason why he had ceased to attend church, that once he heard something there about his Saviour, Jesus Christ, but now all the discourse was about one John Toland." This took place in 1697. In 1700, Berkeley, at the age of fifteen, matriculated at Trinity College.

At the most receptive period of his precocious youth he thus found himself plunged in the middle stream of eighteenth century thought, already running with a full tide though still so near its source. For more than thirty years the character of his speculative writings turned on questions in debate during the period in which he began his first residence at Trinity College. His philosophical batteries are always directed so as to present a threefold opposition to the metaphysics of Locke, certain mathematico-physical assumptions which he ascribed to Newton, and the theological inferences of the Deists and Free-thinkers.

[1] *Religious Thought in England,* vol. ii. p. 244.

But it must never be forgotten that, in his opposition to the new ideas, he did not represent the age that was going out, but (though in a peculiar manner) the age that was coming in. He was not engaged in the last desperate stand made along the old lines, with the old argumentative weapons, against invading innovations. In so far as he opposed the new conclusions, it was in the spirit of the new premises. If he attacked Locke, it was not as a disciple of the schoolmen. If he criticised Newton, it was not as a disciple of Descartes. And, though his orthodoxy was beyond suspicion, we may look through his theological writings in vain for that learned discussion of dogmatic subtleties which was dear to the seventeenth century, of which his own contemporaries produced more than one admirable example, but which was on the whole alien to the taste of the eighteenth century, whether believing or sceptical, whether lay or clerical. It would be a more natural, but not a less important error, to suppose that Berkeley's habits of thought [1] anticipated something of the spirit of the nineteenth century. He is, as

[1] From all these remarks I exclude the *Siris*, the work of his last years, of which I shall have to speak later.

every one knows, an "idealist": and it might be concluded that his speculations had something of the imaginative vagueness which characterised the idealistic reaction against the shallow rationalism of the pre-revolutionary period. But it is not so. Berkeley emphatically belonged to his age. The same impatience of authority in matters of speculation, the same passion for clearness and simplicity, the same dislike of what was either pedantic on the one side or rhetorical on the other, the same desire to clothe his thoughts in an agreeable literary dress, is found in him as in any French philosopher who undertook to acquaint admiring *salons* with the latest phases in the emancipation of reason. His creed, indeed, was different, as were his aims, but he belonged to the same century, intellectually as well as chronologically.

On these and on other points connected with the development of Berkeley's modes of thought, we have most interesting evidence in his *Commonplace Book*, first published by Professor Fraser in 1870; consisting of miscellaneous notes and memoranda entirely connected with his philosophical studies, and jotted down, apparently, between the years

1705-1707, *i.e.* when Berkeley was little more than twenty. That a collection of this kind, never intended to meet any eyes but those of its author, should contain much that is crude and even absurd, that there should be frequent repetition and no method, is, of course, inevitable. A soliloquy from which these characteristics are absent is most surely intended to be overheard. To my taste, therefore, these defects, if defects they be, only add to the vividness, and, therefore, to the interest, of the fragment of intellectual autobiography so fortunately preserved. We have here, in casual and detached utterances, almost the whole substance of the philosophy which, in a form exquisitely polished and developed, Berkeley afterwards gave to the world. But we have much more than this. We are allowed to watch all the emotions which, in the mind of its author, accompanied the birth of the new Idea.[1] His hopes, his fears, his good resolutions, his confidence in the value of his discovery, his misgivings as to its reception, are put before us in the liveliest way in notes of almost ejaculatory brevity, or fragments of dialogue with imaginary opponents.

[1] *i.e.* The non-existence of independent matter.

"I wonder not," he tells us,[1] "at my sagacity in discovering the obvious tho' amazing truth ; I rather wonder at my stupid inadvertency in not finding it out before— 'tis no witchcraft to see."

And again—

MEM.—That I was distrustful at eight years old, and consequently by nature disposed to these new doctrines.[2]

All things in the Scripture which side with the vulgar against the learned, side with me also. I side in all things with the mob. I know there is a mighty sect of men will oppose me, but yet I may expect to be supported by those whose minds are not overgrown with madness.[3]

MEM.—To be eternally banishing Metaphysics, etc., and recalling men to common sense.[4]

My end is not to deliver Metaphysics in a general scholastic way, but in some way to accommodate them to the sciences, etc.[5]

I abstain from all flourish and powers of words and figures, using a great plainness and simplicity of simile, having oft found it difficult to understand those that use the lofty and Platonic or subtil and scholastic strain.[6]

There are some of the notes which might be quoted as being pertinent to the foregoing account of Berkeley's frame of mind while at Trinity College. Let me add to them a maxim which, fortunately for the world, Berkeley only very imperfectly observed, viz. :—

---

[1] *Life and Letters*, p. 489. [2] *Ibid.* p. 488. [3] *Ibid.* p. 420.
[4] *Ibid.* p. 445.   [5] *Ibid.* p. 482. [6] *Ibid.* p. 492.

N.B.—To rein in ye satyrical nature.[1]

And another for which it is strange he should even have thought he had any occasion :—

N.B.—To use utmost caution not to give least offence to the Church or Churchmen.[2]

Possibly, when he penned the last of these admonitions to himself, he was thinking of the wearisome controversy which arose out of the offence given to the too sensitive orthodoxy of Bishop Stillingfleet by Locke's doctrine of substance.

However this may be, Berkeley had no hesitation in openly ranging himself with "the Church and Churchmen"; for within a very short time of his penning the words, namely, in 1709, he took orders, and in the same year, at the age of twenty-four, he gave to the world his first philosophical book—the *New Theory of Vision.* This dealt with but a small number of the problems on which, as the *Commonplace Book* shows, he had for some time arrived at novel and interesting conclusions; but it was rapidly followed by the *Principles of Human Knowledge* (1710), which contain what we are in the habit of calling

[1] *Life and Letters,* p. 433.
[2] *Ibid.* p. 451.

E

the "Berkeleian Philosophy," in a tolerably complete form; while in the next two years were written the dialogue between Hylas and Philonous, which presented his early speculations in their final and most elaborate shape.

Before he was twenty-eight, therefore, Berkeley had finished the work on which his position in the history of philosophy chiefly depends. His life was not half run out, and the part which still remained to him was not only far more full of incident and interest than the few quiet years spent in excogitating his new "Principle" in the studious retirement of Trinity College, but must have seemed to his contemporaries far more reasonably employed. We, on the other hand, shall, perhaps, be rather inclined to wonder that a man who had done so much before he was thirty, had not done much more by the time he was sixty. The precocity of his genius and its comparative barrenness may seem to us almost equal matters of surprise. The strangeness of both, however, diminishes on reflexion. Philosophy is nearly as likely to be done well in early as in later life. It needs neither profound knowledge of human nature, nor that superficial acquaintance with the ways of mankind which goes by the name of "knowledge of the world." It is wholly independent of experience, and nearly independent even of book learning. It scarcely requires, therefore, for its successful cultivation any of the accomplishments, for the full development of which Time is a necessary condition. What it demands from its successful votaries is the instinct which tells them where, along the line of contemporary speculation, that point is to be found from which the next advance may best be made, and that speculative faculty which is as much a natural gift as an aptitude for mathematics or a genius for poetry. Should they lack the first of these requisites, they will be left, whatever their ability, like Berkeley's contemporaries, Clarke and Malebranch, out of the main current of thought in a kind of philosophical back-water; should they lack the second, they have made a mistake as to their true calling, which neither industry nor learning will do anything to remedy. Berkeley possessed both gifts. We need not wonder, therefore, that like many other philosophers—like Hume, Fichte, Schelling, and Schopenhauer—he produced valuable original work at an early age. That he produced so little in his maturer years is doubtless due in part to

temperament, and to the distractions of an unsettled
and wandering life, but it must also be largely
attributed to the almost total absence of intelligent
criticism, either from friends or foes, under which
Berkeley suffered throughout the whole period
during which such criticism might have roused him
to make some serious effort to develop or to defend
the work of his youth.   Professor Fraser has given
us, from unpublished sources, an account of one
ineffectual effort which Berkeley made to get his
views discussed by a competent critic.   In 1711 his
friend Sir John Percival, to whom Berkeley had
applied for information as to the reception of the
Principles, reported that the book had fallen into Dr.
Clarke's hands.   Clarke, it appears, read it, disagreed
with it, but refused to give his reasons ; and was,
moreover, alleged to have expressed an opinion that
Berkeley's labours were " of little use on account of
their abstruseness."   Poor Berkeley, who flattered
himself that his treatise did away with the "chief
causes of error and difficulty in the sciences," and
destroyed the "grounds of scepticism, atheism, and
irreligion," was naturally distressed at a criticism
which, it must be confessed, came with rather an ill

grace from the author of the metaphysical "Demon-
stration of the Being and Attributes of God."   The
rest of the world has so long and so unanimously said
of philosophers that their labours are "useless to
mankind on account of their abstruseness," that
philosophers should in common decency refrain from
saying it of each other.

Berkeley, however, was now to be in a position
to judge for himself, and at first hand, what the
world thought of his system.   Early in January 1713
he gave up his academic life in Dublin, and, with the
manuscript of his unpublished *Dialogues* in his pocket,
started for London.   He was there only seven months.
He had the assistance neither of wealth nor of family
connection, and did not even carry with him, so far
as we know, any powerful recommendations from his
native country ; for the reputation of having written
a book which those who had read it thought useless,
and those who had not, thought mad, can hardly be
so esteemed.[1]   Yet we find him almost immediately
received into the intimate society of the Whig men of
letters, like Steele and Addison, and of the Tory men

---

[1] It is true, however, that Berkeley alleges that Steele was
interested in his account of the *Principles of Human Knowledge*,
and that Arbuthnot was a convert to the *Dialogues*.

of letters, like Swift and Arbuthnot. He was engaged to write in the *Guardian*. Pope presented him with a copy of a "very ingenious new poem," *Windsor Forest*. He went to Court, he was introduced to ministers and statesmen, and finally obtained an appointment as chaplain to a special embassy of Lord Peterborough.

The foundation of this rapid success was doubtless due to Berkeley's extraordinary charm of manner. The effect of this on all who met him seems to have been instantaneous and lasting. The words in which Atterbury recorded his first impression of him are almost as well known as the line in which Pope attributes to him "every virtue under heaven." Less well known, but equally characteristic, is the anecdote which records that he had to escape by stratagem from the hospitality of Wilton, so unwilling was Lord Pembroke to be deprived of the pleasures of his society. But it may be doubted whether any charm of character or manner would, under ordinary circumstances, have so soon produced its natural fruits, even though its possessor had enjoyed in addition the reputation of having written a book which nobody could understand. The explanation is rather to be sought in the fact that while his nationality gained Berkeley an introduction through his countrymen, Steele and Swift, into the best literary society of the day, the best literary society had, in relation to the best society of other kinds, a position in Queen Anne's time which it has never exactly occupied either before or since. Lord Macaulay would have us believe[1] that this was due to the fact that after the Revolution statesmen felt the growing necessity of appealing to public opinion outside the walls of Parliament, and, at a time when debates were conducted with closed doors, could only do so by means of the press: so that, as a natural consequence, men of letters ceased to be merely the objects of their patronage, and became their allies and their associates. That this explanation partly accounts for the facts I am far from denying, but that it does so only in part is clear from the circumstance that the alleged cause existed long after the alleged consequence had disappeared. In the time of Walpole, who valued this kind of assistance so highly that he is said to have spent £50,000 in ten years to secure it, there was no privileged literary circle of any consequence, and no

---

[1] *Essay on Addison.*

men of letters received high political appointments. Moreover, while in the preceding period a writer so useful to ministers, as, for example, Defoe, was paid for his services in hard cash, and not either in posts of distinction or in social consideration, it would be hard, I think, to show that there was more than a very general connection between the political writings and the politico-social successes of such men as Prior, Addison, or even Swift. Prior began the diplomatic career, in which he finally became ambassador and plenipotentiary, in 1690; but I am not aware that he contributed anything but verses to party contro-versy, except some numbers of the *Examiner* in 1710. Addison's political writings are a mere fraction of his works; and if the places and pensions which he at various times obtained are to be considered as a payment for them, it must at all events be admitted that they were a payment conducted on very strange principles. He had received a pension and had been made under-secretary before writing anything political at all. A single pamphlet in defence of the war was followed by his appointment to the Irish Chief Secretaryship. From the time the Whigs went out in 1710, till they came in again on the death of the Queen, he wrote, I believe, but one political pamphlet besides the Whig *Examiner*; and the Whig *Examiner* he discontinued just when the Tory *Examiner*, in Swift's hands, became most formidable. There never was a time when his party was more in need of a powerful pen than during this season of their adversity; but Addison devoted almost all his energies during it to purely literary work, and did his best to dissuade Steele from taking a different course. Yet so far were his friends from thinking that they had reason to complain of his remissness, that on their return to office, they immediately re-appointed him to the Irish Chief Secretaryship. The services which Swift's pen did to his party, it would, indeed, be difficult to overrate. But no one can doubt that, from whatever motives the Tory Ministers began to receive him into a flattering intimacy, they continued to do so not because they wanted to buy him as a writer, but because they valued him as an adviser, and loved him as a friend.

The main cause, therefore, of the unique position of men of letters in the first quarter of the last century, is to be found, I believe, not in any law of social evolution, but in a mere coincidence—in the coincidence, namely, of two men, both in the very first rank of literary ability, both entirely devoid of literary jealousy, both zealous and disinterested friends to their literary brethren, both combining great independence with the rarest social gifts, and both ready to do political as well as literary work— in the coincidence (I say) of two such men existing together at a time when the leaders of both political parties were eminently qualified to appreciate their excellences. When we speak of the men of letters in the age of Queen Anne, we are usually thinking principally of Addison and "his little senate," of Swift and the Scriblerus Club; the rest were "Grub Street," and suffered neither a better nor a worse fate under Queen Anne than under the first Georges. My contention is that the explanation of the un-exampled influence of the former is to be found, not in the mere fact that the statesmen of that day desired to secure the services of writers capable of producing *The Freeholder* or *The Conduct of the Allies*, but in the fact that men like Addison and Swift were contemporaries of men like Somers and Halifax, Oxford and Bolingbroke.

However this may be, and I have perhaps paused

too long over a question which is but indirectly connected with my subject, there is no doubt that Berkeley greatly profited by the state of things he found existing in London. Neither then, nor at any other time, did he mix himself up in party controversy. In ecclesiastical matters he was apparently a moderate High Churchman, in politics a moderate Tory. But at a time when both ecclesiastical and political party feeling ran very high, his interests seem always to have centred in other, broader, and perhaps less practical, issues; and he therefore associated on perfectly easy terms with men whose difference of opinion debarred them from associating on perfectly easy terms with each other. If this circumstance prevented him being an actor in the stormy politics of the period, it enabled him to be an impartial spectator of more than one scene interesting in our literary history. At Easter 1713, Addison's tragedy of *Cato* was acted for the first time. Most people know Macaulay's lively account of this celebrated "first night," though comparatively few know anything else about what was, according to Voltaire, the first "regular" tragedy that had ever been brought on the English stage. The success of the play, so far as success may be measured by applause, was certain from the first. For in the then condition of politics, everybody was determined to find in it a political intention; and as neither party would permit the other to appropriate to itself the fine sentiments with which its speeches abounded, Whig and Tory clapped against one another in noisy but undiscriminating emulation. Pope tells us how the author "sweated behind the scenes with concern to find the applause proceeded more from the hand than the head"; and Berkeley writes that he "was present with Mr. Addison and a few more friends in a side box, where we had a table and two or three flasks of Burgundy and Champagne, with which the author (who is a very sober man) thought it necessary to support his spirits. . . . Lord Harley, who sat in the box next us, was observed to clap as loud as any in the house all the time of the play."[1] The picture is amusing, and the testimony to Addison's habitual sobriety is interesting on account of the accusation of intemperance which has been brought against him.

[1] Bishop Hurd amusingly remarks, in his note to *Cato* : "While the *present humour* of idolising Shakespeare continues, no quarter will be given to this poem."

From another letter which Professor Fraser has
brought to light, and which I cannot resist quoting,
we learn that in March Berkeley breakfasted with
Addison and Swift at the lodgings of the latter.
This incident (which is not mentioned, I believe, in
the Journal to Stella) is interesting, as throwing
light on the relations of two eminent men, whose
friendship was sometime sorely strained, but never
quite broken, by political differences.

"I breakfasted," says Berkeley, "with him [*i.e.* with
Addison] at Dr. Swift's lodgings in Bury Street. His
coming when I was there, and the good temper which he
showed, I construed as a sign of the approaching coalition
of parties. Dr. Swift is admired by both Steele and
Addison, and I think him one of the best-natured and
most agreeable men in the world."

The prophecy suggested in this extract had more
of charity in it than of foresight. Not many months
had passed before "the best-natured man in the
world" was gibbeting Steele in *The Importance of the
"Guardian" considered*. In little more than a year
Swift was an exile in his native land, and the Tory
chiefs were either imprisoned or were flying for their
lives.

Before this wreck of all his hopes Swift was able

to do for Berkeley one of the many kindnesses which, in the days of his power, he conferred on his literary brethren. He got him appointed chaplain to the special embassy of which the celebrated Lord Peterborough was the head. The service he thus did his friend was greater than may at first appear. In the last century, travelling meant something more than hurrying through picture galleries, staring at churches, and seeing a little of everything in foreign countries except their inhabitants. But while its advantages were greater, so also was its cost. A man, without introductions or powerful connections, could not enjoy its full benefits; and a man without money, or the assistance of those who had money, could scarcely hope to enjoy them at all. Under these circumstances, there were two methods by which a poor man might obtain direct knowledge of foreign society or foreign art. He might become companion, probably tutor, to some richer person, or he might obtain an appointment on some embassy. Addison, Gray, Adam Smith, are examples of the first method; Locke and Hume of the second. Berkeley enjoyed both. In 1713-14, as chaplain to Lord Peterborough's mission, from 1716-20, as tutor

to the son of Ashe, Bishop of Clogher, he travelled
on the Continent under favourable circumstances,
visiting France, Italy, and Sicily.

It is not necessary to pause over his wanderings.
Of part of them we have a very full record in a
journal which has been preserved, and which Professor Fraser has, for the first time, rendered
accessible. From this it is easy to discern the spirit
in which he wandered through Italy and Sicily,
lingering with delight in what he describes, in an
admirable letter to Pope, as the "romantic" scenery
of Ischia, or penetrating into the little-known recesses
of Calabria. He does not indulge largely in historical
or political reflections, nor are his pages loaded with
classical reminiscences, though these are not wanting;
but he notes the external aspect of the country and
its inhabitants, the character of the agriculture, of
the scenery, and, even more particularly, of the
architecture. He is, besides, a keen scientific
investigator. He sent home to Arbuthnot, and
Arbuthnot communicated to the Royal Society, an
excellent account of an ascent of Vesuvius during an
eruption. He inquired with great care, though with
no very conclusive result, into the phenomena of

Tarantism—*i.e.* into the effects that were supposed
to follow the bite of the Tarantula ; and he made a
collection of the flora of Sicily.   All this has for us
now only a biographical interest; and even if the
second part of the *Principles of Human Knowledge,*
which he wrote in Sicily, and which was lost at sea,
had been preserved, it may be doubted whether much
of permanent value would have been added to what
we know of his philosophy from other sources.   But
it cannot be doubted that the effect of his travels
on Berkeley himself was great, and that when he
returned to England at the end of 1720, he brought
back from the Continent a knowledge of men and
things, and a cultivated sensibility to the beauties of
nature and art, which have left permanent traces in
his writings.

The inner connection of the events which occurred
in the three years immediately succeeding his return
home are, at first sight, difficult to discover.   But
the events themselves are easily told.   He arrived in
England during the very crisis of the South Sea
mania.   This, and what else he saw of the condition
of society, startled him into writing an *Essay towards
the Prevention of the Ruin of Great Britain,* of which it

is sufficient to say here that it is one of those energetic protests against national vices to which no nation, standing gravely in need of it, would be likely to pay much attention. This done, and acquaintance renewed with the survivors among his old literary friends, he seems to have laid himself out for ecclesiastical preferment. The architectural knowledge acquired in Italy recommended him to the architectural Lord Burlington, through whose influence he became chaplain to the Duke of Grafton, then just appointed Lord-Lieutenant of Ireland. The post seems to have been little to Berkeley's liking, But if, as is probable, he accepted it as a step to one more congenial to his tastes, he certainly succeeded better than his friend Swift, who had occupied a similar position with similar hopes many years before, but with no better reward than the living of Laracor. The more fortunate Berkeley was appointed, in rapid succession, by his College to several lectureships, and by the Lord-Lieutenant to a living and two deaneries. The deanery of Dromore, on account of some legal obstacle, he seems never to have enjoyed. With regard to the deanery of Derry there were no such difficulties. But he had no sooner

F

entered into undisturbed possession of it than he astonished his friends by expressing the most ardent wish to leave it, in order to execute a scheme for the conversion of America.

It certainly seems strange at first sight that Berkeley should thus for some years have sought ecclesiastical preferment with no other apparent object than to resign it as soon as it was obtained. But the fact seems to be that during those years his scheme of life underwent a complete change. Doubtless, he returned, after his long wanderings, anxious for a settled home and determinate work, and with the intention of finding these in the ordinary development of a clerical career. But the spectacle of the corrupt society of the early Georgian period, rendered more repulsive by the shameless fraud and avarice that accompanied the South Sea speculation, shocked his unaccustomed gaze. He conceived a profound dislike of a civilisation eaten into, and, as he believed, fatally undermined, by idleness, self-indulgence, and irreligion. He turned, as others in a like position have turned, to a younger and a more hopeful society across the ocean. There gradually grew up in his mind the strange but fascinating dream of a missionary college, which should be a centre of civilisation to the rising Empire in the West. His imagination filled itself with the vision of a learned and devout company of friends, far removed from luxury and the snares which beset the search for wealth, devoting themselves, under the serene skies of Bermuda, to the instruction of native Americans, who were in their turn to teach their brethren on the mainland those truths of Christian morality which in Europe men continued to profess, but had long ceased to value. If, however, the vision was to become a reality, the first and most important step was to convince a sceptical age of his own unselfish belief in its possibility. And it may well have seemed to Berkeley that, as a means towards attaining this end, he could not do better than obtain that ecclesiastical preferment which he had probably originally sought from other and more ordinary motives. A missionary scheme which would have received scant attention while advocated by a literary clergyman of no established position, unsupported by any powerful connection, might wear a very different complexion when promoted by a dean who was prepared to sacrifice his deanery to assist it. A man who was not only ready, but anxious to give up two thousand

a year at home in order to get a hundred a year in
the middle of the Atlantic, might be visionary, but
must certainly be disinterested; and Berkeley knew
well enough that in order to get people to believe in
his scheme, it was first necessary to make them
believe in himself.

If this was his object, it must be admitted that,
in the first instance at least, it was thoroughly
attained. His unrivalled powers of personal persuasion were unsparingly used to further his cause.
Every one knows the anecdote narrated by Warton,
on the authority of Lord Bathurst, which tells how
the members of the Scriblerus Club agreed to rally
Berkeley on his project, how, after hearing all that
they had to say, he asked to be heard in his turn,
and how the eloquence of the philanthropic philosopher so moved them, that those who came to scoff
remained to subscribe. The story, though strange,
may be believed, since we have it on no less evidence
than the Statute Book, that he performed the far
more amazing feat of obtaining a grant of money
(£20,000) from the State, and this at a time when
Sir Robert Walpole was responsible for its finances.
Nobody was more surprised at such a result than Sir

Robert himself, who attributed it, and with good reason, not to the merits of the project, but to the persuasive powers of the projector. These were, in truth, used without stint. The King's Court at St. James's and the Princes' Court at Leicester Fields, the world of letters and the world of fashion, as well as every individual member of the House of Commons, were canvassed on behalf of the scheme, and with such effect that, as we have seen, the nation promised money, the King granted a charter, Walpole himself subscribed, Bermuda became the fashion, and even Bolingbroke talked of emigrating, *not* in a missionary capacity, to Berkeley's ideal island.

Yet the scheme seems now so impracticable, that we may well wonder how any single person, let alone the representatives of a whole nation, could be found to support it. In order that religion and learning might flourish in America, the seeds of them were to be cast in some rocky islets severed from America by nearly six hundred miles of stormy ocean. In order that the inhabitants of the mainland and of the West Indian colonies might equally benefit by the new university, it was to be placed in such a position that neither could conveniently reach it. In order that no taint of luxury should corrupt its morals, it was to be removed far from every source of wealth and every centre of industry to a place where, as Berkeley flattered himself, there was no more lucrative occupation possible than that of making straw hats. It was to spring from no natural want, it was to follow no natural growth, it was to be thrown as it were from without to a population which had never expressed any desire for it, and in whom a desire was not likely to be excited by a gift which, however valuable in itself, was presented to them for the first time in so singular and so inconvenient a shape.

Berkeley, it may be observed, was not moved to adopt his scheme by any such Utopian views, either of the European colonists or the native Americans, as became fashionable on the Continent at a later period of the century. He did not believe that a society which, by force of circumstances, was free from the vices incident to an ancient and complex civilisation was therefore virtuous; nor yet that in hordes of ignorant savages was to be found the perfect and uncorrupted work of Nature. On the contrary, in the curious pamphlet in which he recommended his project to the public, he expressly

mentions the "avarice, the licentiousness, the cold-
ness in the practice of religion, and the aversion from
propagating it," of which the colonists on the mainland were accused; and tells us that "no part of the
Gentile world are so inhuman and barbarous as the
savage Americans, whose chief employment and
delight consist in cruelty and revenge." But he
certainly believed that in the New World there was
not only the largest, but also the most hopeful field
for missionary effect. Society there might be corrupt,
but it was not, like society in Europe, grown old in
corruption. The native Indians might be ignorant
and brutal, but "if they were unimproved by education, they were also unencumbered with that rubbish
of superstition and prejudice which is the effect of a
wrong one." He imagined that if only the religion
and learning of the Old World, purified from its
pedantry and its vice, could be brought to bear on
the New while this was yet young and plastic, the
eyes of posterity might be gladdened by the sight of
a new Golden Age; and he bursts into a strain of
almost prophetic rapture as, in vigorous verses, he
describes the new Arts and new Empire, "not such
as Europe breeds in her decay," which were to

rise in the West, the "last and noblest" birth of Time.

Reflections such as these suggested, we may be sure, the main outlines of his scheme. The character of its details was probably due to his special idiosyncrasies. Ten years before, in one of his papers in the *Guardian*, he had drawn a picture of University life as it might be, as it had been, perhaps, to him, but as it certainly was not, in his day, to the majority of students. The same vision haunted his declining years. And doubtless, while still in the prime of life, a project which should enable him to further the interests of a continent, while holding himself aloof, in academic retirement, from the noise, the dust, and the contamination of the struggling multitude, had, as it might well have, irresistible fascination. But this was not all. His fancy lingered lovingly over the picture drawn by poets and travellers of the scenery in the western isles. With Ischia and Sicily still fresh in his recollection, he dwelt on the orange-groves and cedars, the cloudless skies, and the perpetual spring which were to be found in Bermuda. He even dreamed of rearing amid these natural beauties collegiate buildings, which his architectural knowledge should render not unworthy of their setting.

The vision, it must be owned, was a fascinating one; but it was never to be realised, even in the smallest particular. Fortunately, as I hold, for Berkeley, his scheme was not even tried sufficiently to show its incurable vices. In pursuance of his mission, he left England, it is true, in 1728 with his newly-married wife, but he never reached Bermuda. In Rhode Island, where he arrived after a long and tedious passage, he waited, perhaps with diminishing belief in his own plans, for the funds which never came. Sir Robert Walpole had been forced by an unexpected vote to promise a sum of twenty thousand pounds, but there was nothing to force him to pay it. "If you put the question to me as a Minister," he said, "I can assure you that the money shall most undoubtedly be paid—as soon as suits public convenience; but if you ask me as a friend whether Dean Berkeley shall continue in America expecting the payment of £20,000, I advise him by all means to return to Europe."

To Europe accordingly Berkeley returned. Of Bermuda we hear no more. But he long retained a

lively interest in the colony in which for nearly three
years he had, as it were by accident, found a home.
To Yale and to Harvard colleges he sent, soon after
his arrival in England, a gift of books; and to the
former he left his farm near Newport (the scenery of
which he has so exquisitely described in *Alciphron*)
for the perpetual sustentation of three scholarships.
The foundation exists, I believe, to the present day,
and has not only served the purpose for which it
was immediately founded, but has aided the education
of some of those who have most earnestly devoted
themselves to raising the condition of the North
American Indians.   This is the only contribution
which Berkeley has made to the cause for which he
left England ; and it is, perhaps, the most permanent and important result of an enterprise begun
with vast aims and lofty hopes, the record of which
remains, indeed, a splendid testimony to the personal
charm, to the self-forgetful zeal, to the disinterested
benevolence of its author; but also a standing proof
of how little in the region of action these high
qualities avail, dissociated from the practical instinct
which distinguishes between what does and what does
not deserve to be attempted.

IF Berkeley's journey to America did not materially further the object for which it was undertaken, it was not, on the other hand, wholly barren of results. During the three years of enforced but agreeable leisure which he spent in Rhode Island, he composed the longest, and, in his own lifetime, the most considered of all his writings—*Alciphron, or the Minute Philosopher*.

This work—a series of seven dialogues directed against the Deists—contains Berkeley's chief polemical contribution to the great religious controversy of his generation. During the thirty-seven years that intervened between the publication of Toland's *Christianity not Mysterious* and that of *Alciphron*, this controversy had never flagged. But, though the points in debate are not widely removed from those which profoundly stir men's interests now, they are just sufficiently removed to make the discussion of them empty and unsatisfactory to modern ears. Objections to revealed religion founded upon textual criticism, history, and science, were put then as they are put now, but they were put and answered by men to whom criticism, history, and science, in the modern use of those terms, were practically unknown. The consequence of this has been that, with the one exception of Butler's *Analogy*, the merely argumentative part of that voluminous controversy has lost all but a historic interest, and only those fragments of it can now be read with pleasure which are preserved from neglect by their purely literary merits.

This is hard upon the Deists; for, whatever may have been the intrinsic strength of their arguments, it is generally admitted that all the wit (to say nothing of the learning) was on the side of their opponents. Their writings are now antiquated, but they were always dull; and there is scarcely a single piece deliberately intended to further their distinctive opinions which can now be read with any sort of satisfaction. The fact is remarkable. In an age in which so large a proportion of the best literary work, whether in prose or verse, was satirical; in which even those who, like Gray and Akenside, would least have desired to be remembered as satirists seemed to write with unwonted ease and vigour when they trespassed on satiric ground, it is strange that no one could be found able and willing to retaliate in kind on the attacks of Swift, Steele, Bentley, and Berkeley. Even Pope, whose *Essay on Man* was mainly founded on the writings of one Deist and the conversations of another, has nothing but sneers for the "smart freethinker," and took occasion to pillory their most considerable authors in the *Dunciad*; while Shaftesbury, though he loudly recommended the use of ridicule as a cure for "enthusiasm" and "superstition," was, unfortunately, denied by nature the gifts necessary for supplementing his precepts by his example. It was not till Deism had been transplanted from its original home to the more congenial soil of France, that the balance was redressed. Voltaire, who added little to the argumentative armoury of Collins, Tindal, and the rest, for the first time succeeded in making infidelity amusing, while, unlike his English predecessors, he met with nothing in the field of literature deserving the name of resistance.

Berkeley, it will be recollected, had been interested

from his earliest Dublin days in the Deistic controversy. The very title pages of his *Principles of
Human Knowledge*, and of the *Dialogue of Hylas and
Philonous*, proclaimed the fact that his philosophic
speculations were intended as a remedy for "Scepticism," "Atheism," and "Irreligion." But he soon found
that his remedy, whatever might be its intrinsic value,
was scarcely adapted for general use.   Ordinary men
were not prepared to admit that a Deity was necessary
because matter was impossible.   In the *Guardian* he
accordingly adopted a more popular style, well suited
to readers who knew little of theology and nothing of
metaphysics, but who required to be reminded that
religion had some claims to the gratitude and reverence of mankind, and that the pretensions of those
who attacked it provided no measure of their merits.

Who, then, were these enemies of religion? By
their opponents they were not unfrequently described
as persons who, in matters practical, were of relaxed
morals, and in matters speculative might be called
almost indifferently Deists, freethinkers, and atheists.
Yet nothing is more certain than that Shaftesbury,
for instance, and Collins, were perfectly respectable
members of society, and that while all the more

important writers on the unorthodox side would have repudiated the name of atheist, Shaftesbury, at least, made ardent and, doubtless, sincere professions of Theism. Are we then to attribute the language of the orthodox party to the mere heat and prejudice of controversy? In part, I think, we must. The almost incredible coarseness with which, under cover of a learned tongue, men of learning and piety had in preceding ages not unfrequently conducted their disputes, was in the eighteenth century greatly mitigated. But the practice of exaggerating the errors of an opponent, in order to gibbet them with more effect, prevailed to a serious extent. The High Churchman was denounced as a Papist. The Low, or (as we should now say) Broad Churchman, was denounced as a Latitudinarian; the Latitudinarian was denounced as a Socinian; the Socinian as a Deist; the Deist as an atheist. But, admitting all this, it must be remembered that it would be most unjust to estimate the controversial moderation of the orthodox divines in the first half of the last century, by a bare comparison of their language with the official utterances of their opponents. Berkeley, especially, can never be understood, unless we keep in mind that he interpreted the text of Shaftesbury, Collins, and Mandeville by the light of the social facts of his own day. The Deist movement did not appear to him as it does to us, in the form of a certain number of treatises directed against the received theology, for the most part tedious, of slight literary merit, containing nothing either to agitate or instruct the modern reader, and predestined, in England at least, to bear little permanent fruit. In his view, these were rather the more prominent and public signs of a widespread attack on religion, conducted orally on much more extreme lines, and with great and growing success. He believed in the existence of freethinking clubs, where those who, in their published writings were content to advocate Deism, professed in private to demonstrate that no Deity could possibly exist. He believed that Society was honeycombed with a religious scepticism, not arising from any disinterested pursuit of truth, but from mere libertinism in thought, at once the effect and the cause of libertinism in conduct; and he traced a direct connection between the relaxed morality of the Georgian era and the contemptous tone towards Christianity rendered fashionable by the Deistical writers.

The consequence of this is that, while his contemporary, Butler, addresses himself entirely to producing a convincing reply to the formal arguments of the freethinkers, Berkeley seeks also to attack them on what we may term their social side. His strokes are aimed not only at Shaftesbury and Collins, but at the Coffee-house infidels;—the would-be men of fashion, who thought that there was no greater proof of enlightenment than to sneer at Christianity, or of wit than to cut jokes on a parson. He is never weary of dilating on the pretentious ignorance of these gentlemen.

"Who," says Euphranor (one of the orthodox speakers in *Alciphron*), "are these profound and learned men that of late years have demolished the whole fabric which philosophers, lawgivers, and divines have been erecting for so many ages?"

Lysicles (the infidel man of fashion), hearing these words, smiled, and said that he believed Euphranor had figured to himself philosophers in square caps and long gowns; but, thanks to these happy times, the reign of pedantry is over. "Our philosophers," said he, "are of a different kind from those awkward students. . . . I will undertake a lad of fourteen, bred in the modern way, shall make a better figure and be more considered in any drawing-room than one of four-and-twenty, who hath lain by a long time at school or college. He shall say better

G

things, in a better manner, and be more liked by good judges."

Euphranor.—"Whence doth he pick up all this improvement ?"

Crito (ironically).—"Where our grave ancestors would never have looked for it—in a drawing-room, a coffee-house, a chocolate-house, at the tavern or groom porters."

And so forth.

To us, who are directly acquainted with nothing but the literary remains of the controversy, the laugh seems so clearly to be on the side of Orthodoxy, that we have some difficulty in recollecting that to Berkeley and Berkeley's contemporaries the fact must have seemed exactly reversed. The "raillery" which Shaftesbury recommended as the test of truth was, in society, freely employed against "priestcraft" in general, and the clergy of the Established Church in particular; who, when not denounced as bigots, were ridiculed as musty pedants.

"I have often observed," says Crito, "that the Free-thinking sect run into two faults of conversation, declaiming and bantering, just as the tragic or comic humour prevails. Sometimes they work themselves into a high passion, and are frightened at spectres of their own raising. In those fits every country curate passes for an inquisitor. At other times they affect a sly, facetious manner, expressing little, insinuating much, and upon the whole seeming to divert themselves with the subject and their adversaries." "Can no method be found," he exclaims in a later dialogue, "to free them from the terror of that fierce and bloody animal, an English parson?"

Arguments may be refuted, but "who," it has been asked, "can answer a sneer?" Berkeley in *Alciphron* attempted to answer both the arguments and the sneer. It was this double object which probably induced him to employ the most difficult of all forms of composition to manage with effect—the Dialogue. He had already, it is true, used it with extraordinary skill in the region of pure exposition. The three dialogues between Hylas and Philonous have never in their peculiar style been equalled in English; they will, I suppose, never be surpassed. Yet what reader, anxious rather to get at the substance of Berkeley's doctrine, than to spend his time over a literary luxury, would not prefer to these admirable conversations the straightforward statement contained in the *Principles of Human Knowledge?* But in the case of *Alciphron*, its author pursued a more complex end. *There* dialogue was not merely one of the two possible forms by which his aim could be reached; it was the only possible form. It was only by bringing his opponents actually on the stage, by dramatising their conversation, by exhibiting the weaknesses of their character as well as the errors of their logic, that his intention could be accomplished in all its fulness. To my thinking, Berkeley was wonderfully successful. Mr. Leslie Stephen, indeed, declares *Alciphron* to be the "least admirable of all its author's admirable works." But I cannot help thinking that this excellent critic, in forming his judgment, was thinking rather of what he desired to find in the book, than of what its author desired to put into it. It may at once be granted that *Alciphron* is not, like the *Analogy*, a great original contribution to theology. Many portions of it are now wholly antiquated ; many other portions contain arguments which have since, by frequent repetition, become the mere commonplaces of apologetics. But there remains more than one admirable application of Berkeley's peculiar philosophy to the theory of religion ; there remain the slight but exquisite descriptions of incident and scenery which form the setting of the piece ; and there remains, above all, the literary skill displayed in the dramatic and polemical elements of the dialogue and in the art with which these are woven together into an organic whole.

It was an inevitable defect in the structure of the piece that, as all the varieties of the genus Freethinker are represented in it by two persons, unity of character cannot be sustained throughout the seven dialogues. Nothing, for instance, can make it natural for Lysicles, the freethinking man of pleasure, who says in one place—

For my part, I find no fault with the Universities; all I know is that I had the spending of three hundred pounds a year in one of them, and think it the cheerfullest time of my life. As for their books and style, I had not leisure to mind them—

nothing, I say, can make it natural for such a man to quote, as he does in another dialogue, Spinoza and Hobbes, and to argue about the metaphysical doctrine of substance. But this is a trifling defect. A far more serious charge has been brought against Berkeley by Sir James Mackintosh, and, more recently, by Professor Fowler in his excellent biography of Shaftesbury, to the effect that, in the third dialogue and elsewhere, the latter has been treated with gross unfairness. I admit at once that

Professor Fowler is right in saying that Berkeley does not examine Shaftesbury's doctrines in the spirit "which befits one philosopher examining the works of another." But I cannot admit that, in Sir James Mackintosh's phrase, he "sinks to the level of a railing polemic."

Shaftesbury is not, to me at least, an attractive writer. His constant efforts to figure simultaneously as a fine gentleman and a fine writer, are exceedingly irritating; and the very moderate success which has attended his efforts in the latter character, suggests the doubt, justified by his general style, whether he can really have shone in the former. His pretensions to taste are quite unjustified by what we know of his opinions. Like most of his contemporaries he despised Gothic architecture, yet he saw nothing to admire in Wren; while he theorised about painting till he persuaded himself that the merits of a picture were wholly independent of its colouring. At the same time it must be acknowledged that eminent authorities have found in him distinguished merits. Mr. Leslie Stephen tells us, that "on the rude stock of commonplace Whiggism he grafted accomplishments strange to most of his countrymen."

He reminded Warburton of Plato, and has been so fortunate as to remind Professor Fowler of Marcus Aurelius. Moreover, by writers on Moral Philosophy he is naturally and properly regarded as a moral philosopher who occupies an important position in the history of ethical speculation as the predecessor of Butler and Hutcheson, the originator of a new method of procedure in moral inquiries.

But Berkeley, it must be recollected, regarded the author of the *Characteristics* from a very different point of view. He was not concerned with the ethical system, which may with more or less success be extracted from these very unsystematic essays; nor yet with the hints contained in them, which have in other hands become important in the history of thought. His interest in Shaftesbury's writings was practical, not speculative. He looked at them not as "one philosopher examining the works of another," but as a man profoundly interested in the actual condition of religious thought must look at a book by which that condition was powerfully affected. It was the general tendency of the theological parts of the *Characteristics*, therefore, and not the special doctrines which might be supported by isolated

passages in them, that moved him to attack Shaftesbury : and I do not think that the account he gives
of that tendency, though perhaps one-sided, is justly
chargeable with gross unfairness.   If, however, it be
alleged that Berkeley has, for controversial purposes,
credited Shaftesbury with holding opinions which the
latter has distinctly repudiated : I reply that Shaftesbury has no right to complain of any critic who
appeals from specific statements in his writings to
their general *animus*, since he himself has never
scrupled to make professions of respect for theological
dogmas which we know him to have held in contempt.

I cannot admit, therefore, that Berkeley is guilty
nearly to the full extent of the charge made against
him ; and I must also point out that, if I read his
character aright, and if the account I have given of
his intentions in writing *Alciphron* be true, Shaftesbury must, of all writers, have been the one he found
most difficult to treat in a spirit of perfect charity.
Berkeley, partly from a natural feeling of *esprit de
corps*, and partly from a higher motive, strongly
objected to the tone adopted towards the clergy in
some sections of society.   Shaftesbury speaks of
them with all the airs of superiority which a " free

writer" and a wit in those days thought himself justified in using towards "pedants" and "bigots." Berkeley was weighed down with a sense of the wickedness and corruptions of his generation. Shaftesbury's creed was a shallow optimism. Berkeley, intent upon the regeneration of the lowest and most brutal of mankind, felt keenly that the forces arrayed on the side of virtue were all too weak as they stood ; and that they did but a small service to morality who, by undermining a belief in a system of future rewards and punishments, "while they extolled the beauty of virtue, attempted to lessen her dower." [1] Shaftesbury, on the other hand, strong in the possession of £10,000 a year, and a feeble constitution, really talks sometimes as if virtue was mainly an object of æsthetic sensibility ; certain on its own merits to be appreciated by gentlemen of "taste and breeding," but sadly injured, from the point of view of Art, by superfluous references to Heaven and Hell.

Nor was Berkeley's opposition to the sentiment of the elder author likely to be softened by admiration for his style.   In *Alciphron* he levels more than one

[1] Essay in the *Guardian*.

sarcasm at it ; and it must be admitted that Shaftesbury's laborious struggles after an "easy way" of
writing, his vulgar affectation of refinement, his
strange experiments in search of the sublime, and the
pedantic trifling which does duty in his writings for
"raillery and humour," were not likely to be more
agreeable to a man of Berkeley's literary taste, than
were Shaftesbury's opinions to a man of Berkeley's
religious convictions.

Two years after the appearance of *Alciphron*
occurred the last great change in the external circumstances of its author. He was appointed to the
Bishopric of Cloyne, through the influence of Queen
Caroline. This remarkable woman, wife of George
II., and by far the most distinguished Queen Consort
England has ever possessed, not content with being,
next to Walpole, the greatest political power in the
country, amused her leisure hours by dabbling in all
the theological and philosophical controversies of the
period. Berkeley, in the days when he was canvass-
ing for his Bermuda scheme, had been obliged to
discuss in her presence, and presumably for her
amusement, his philosophical tenets with Clarke, not,
as he pathetically observed, because he loved Courts,

but because he loved America. Clarke himself, till his death in 1729, was constantly in her society, and but for his scruples respecting the Athanasian doctrine of the Trinity, which permitted him, apparently, to hold a rectory but not to accept a bishopric, would long before, through her favour, have obtained high ecclesiastical preferment. Butler, who a little later than this succeeded to Clarke's position with the Queen, was by her recommendation raised to the See of Bristol. When I add that she caused the whole of the controversy between Clarke and Leibnitz to pass through her hands, it will be seen that few persons—not philosophers—have ever taken a keener or more practical interest in the philosophy of their day. How far she was really competent, by study or natural aptitude, for such inquiries, it is hard to say. She was supposed, perhaps on insufficient evidence, to be unsettled, if not unorthodox, in her religious convictions. If so, it is possible that, like many others in similar circumstances, she was driven to investigation, for which she was perfectly unfitted, by the hope of there finding an anodyne for an unquiet spirit. Horace Walpole,[1] who represents

[1] "The Bishop of Durham (Chandler) is dead : he is succeeded

the social tradition respecting her, declares that she was incapable of understanding Butler's *Analogy*. Clarke, on the other hand, professed a high admiration for her philosophic capacity. The evidence of neither witness is very satisfactory. Clarke was too good a courtier to be a very good judge; while Walpole and his set would certainly be unwilling to believe that any one, much less any woman, least of all any Queen, could find a meaning in abstract arguments which they themselves had never taken the trouble to understand. However this may be, it is unquestionably to her enlightened patronage that the Churches of England and Ireland owed the two most distinguished bishops of the eighteenth century. The appointment of Berkeley is the more creditable, since he had nothing but his merits to recommend him, and was quite unprovided with any of the ordinary titles to Irish ecclesiastical preferment. If he belonged to either Party in the State, he was a Tory; and in Tories who were not Jacobites the

by Butler of Bristol, a metaphysic author, much patronised by the late Queen. She never could make my father read his book, and which she certainly did not understand herself: he told her his religion was fixed, and that he did not want to change or improve it."—Walpole to Mann.

Government saw little either to love or to fear. He was wholly unfitted by taste, character, and abilities, for carrying out the political functions sometimes so strangely associated with the Episcopal office in Ireland. And, besides all this, he had powerful enemies near the person of the Queen; for Hoadley, her favourite bishop, and Lord Hervey, her favourite courtier, liked neither him nor his writings, which, indeed, it must be owned, they were very little fitted to comprehend.

Berkeley's eighteen years of recluse life in his diocese of Cloyne give little material to the biographer. It was a period marked by declining health and increasing infirmities, loss of friends and of children; nor was there anything in the condition of public affairs, either in England or in Ireland, to lighten the burden of these private afflictions. Yet he seems to have been on the whole not unhappy. The glimpses we get of his home life are not very numerous, but they are attractive; the studious retirement which he loved he could indulge in to his heart's content; and though disease and advancing years had sapped the natural energy of his character, he could still on occasion show something of the old fire. We find him, for instance, in 1745, when the Pretender was on his march to Derby, and when fears were naturally entertained lest Ireland should catch the contagion of rebellion from the sister island, writing thus to Dean Gervais :—

Our Militia have been arrayed, that is, sworn : but, alas ! we want not oaths, we want muskets. I have bought up all I could get, and provided horses and arms, for four and twenty of the Protestants of Cloyne, which with a few men, etc.

Two episodes there are, however, in these un-eventful years, to which more particular allusion must be made: the publication of the *Querist* (1735-37) and the *Tar Water* enthusiasm, which followed soon after.

The *Querist*, as my readers are probable aware, is, to all intents and purposes, an essay on the social state of Ireland thrown into the form of a series of questions. Of all the mass of literature which has been devoted to the distresses of that distressful country, this is probably the most original. Its form alone would seem to distinguish it from every other production of a similar kind. It consists of 595 interrogatories, averaging three or four lines in length, and entirely without connecting passages. Sustained eloquence under these conditions is clearly out of the question. It is difficult to understand by what literary arts such a production can even be made readable. Yet readable it certainly is ; and not only readable, but impressive. Berkeley has, in truth, chosen his instrument with remarkable skill. He was enabled by its peculiarities to give his argument on certain rather dry subjects—banks, for instance, and paper currency—with a brevity which no other form of literary composition would have permitted, and a force which in no other form could have been excelled ; while his opinions on the state of the nation lose nothing either by the conciseness with which they are expressed, or the interrogatory form into which they are thrown. Paragraphs like these, for example, serve Berkeley's purpose as well as a whole page of sensational description :—

19. Whether the bulk of our Irish peasantry are not kept from thriving by that cynical content in dirt and beggary which they possess to a degree beyond any other in Christendom ?

456. Whether it be not certain that the matrons of this forlorn country send out a greater proportion of its

wealth for fine apparel than any other females on the whole surface of this terraqueous globe?

106. Whether the dirt, famine, and nakedness of the bulk of our people might not be remedied, even though we had no foreign trade?

132. Whether there be upon earth any Christian or civilised people so beggarly wretched, and destitute, as the common Irish?

133. Whether, nevertheless, there is any other people whose wants may be more easily supplied from home?

Many of the "queries" are, it must be added, enlivened by Berkeley's peculiar turn of irony; for example :—

111. Whether the women (of Ireland) may not sew, spin, weave, embroider, sufficiently for the embellishment of their persons, *and even enough to raise envy in each other*, without being beholden to foreign countries?

330. What right an eldest son hath to the worst education?

405. Whether an expense in building and improvement doth not remain at home, pass to the heir, and adorn the public? *And whether any of these things can be said of claret?*

Yet this method of writing was not without its dangers. It lent itself with unfortunate facility to the intellectual habits which increasing infirmities were bringing on Berkeley. As in *Siris*, of which I shall presently speak, there are hints and adumbrations of a new philosophy strangely tacked on to reflections upon a new medicine; so in the *Querist* there are fragments of a new political economy mixed up with schemes for the social regeneration of Ireland. And it is, I think, clear that in both cases the fragmentary methods of exposition were in part chosen because the ideas to be expounded, though fruitful and original, and though in other hands they have since received a fuller development, were, in the minds of their author, themselves fragmentary and ill-compacted.   Take, as an example of this, Berkeley's opinion upon what is called the "mercantile theory" of commerce—the theory which taught that a nation is benefited by a foreign trade in proportion as that trade brought money or bullion into the country. This absurd doctrine is absolutely exploded in the *Querist*, it is demonstrated to be wrong in theory and wrong in practice; yet some of the queries (*e.g.* 161-2) seem to assume its truth.   Again, nothing can be more explicit than Berkeley's proof that, for currency purposes, notes and gold may perform exactly the same function.   Yet so great is his hatred of the doctrine that money is a source of wealth that, though anxious to increase the amount

H

of the circulation in the country, he is unwilling to increase the amount of gold, and seems almost to hold that, though notes may be a substitute for coin, coin is not a substitute for notes.[1]

My business, however, is not with Berkeley's political economy, any more than with his philosophy, but rather with the temper and qualities of the man himself; and if we would see how these make themselves felt in the treatment of the Irish problem, let us compare the *Querist* with Swift's tracts on Ireland which appeared in the preceding decade. In their diagnosis of the diseases under which that unhappy country was suffering, these two eminent friends agreed with each other, and with the majority of subsequent observers. The idleness, squalor, and poverty of the "native Irish," the absence of manufactures, the ignorance and extravagance of the gentry, their want of care for the real interests of their tenantry and their country,—these are topics common to both. It is when they set themselves to make straight the crooked ways that the difference between them appears. Berkeley tells his countrymen that the remedy for the evils under which they suffer lies,

---

[1] Cf. *Querist*, 227, 283.

in the main, in their own hands.   Let the upper
classes give up a stupid and tasteless extravagance.
Let their women buy fewer silks and laces, and their
men drink less claret.   Let luxury be checked, if
need be, by sumptuary laws.   Let the "standard of
comfort" of the peasantry be raised, and thereby
something done to destroy their lazy contentment in
an existence more squalid and wretched than that of
the savage Americans.   Let manufacturing enterprise
be stimulated by an improved currency, an improved
machinery of credit, and by the increase of a home
demand for home products.   But let nobody imagine
that any good was done by sitting down and
complaining of the tyranny of England.   Though it
were true that England had hampered their commerce
and destroyed their woollen trade, yet nations
had flourished, and were flourishing, whose external
trade was insignificant.   England and Ireland were
one nation, and what was good for the part was good
for the whole.   If Englishmen had forgotten this
truth as regards Irishmen, let not Irishmen forget it
either as regards Englishmen or as regards each other.
Foreign commerce was not necessary to the solid well-
being of the country.   But it *was* necessary that the

manufacturers of the North should not be jealous of the manufacturers of the South; that the landlord should not suppose that he could be prosperous when the tenantry was squalid and miserable; that the Protestant minority should not suppose that they could be rich and flourishing when the Roman Catholic majority were poor and oppressed.

Whatever may be thought of Berkeley's specific proposal, it will not be denied that he treated his subject in the spirit of true patriotism and sound wisdom. So did not Swift. He detested Ireland; he never called himself an Irishman; he would never have set foot in Ireland could he have avoided it. But if he was an Irishman by the visitation of Heaven, he was a partisan by the very necessity of his nature. As a Tory, he hated the Whigs. As an Anglican, he hated both the Irish Roman Catholics and the Irish Presbyterians. As a member of the Lower House of Convocation, he hated the Bishops. As a member of the dominant race he would doubtless have hated the native population had they been formidable enough to provoke any sentiment stronger than a pitying contempt. And so, when compelled to become an

Irishman, it was inevitable that he should also become an Irish patriot.

Irish patriotism took the form then, as it has often done since, not so much of helping Ireland as of thwarting England ; and, doubtless, the task of thwarting England was doubly agreeable to Swift because England meant primarily the Whig Ministry and the commercial classes, who were at once the chief support of the Whigs and the greatest curse to Ireland.   Like Berkeley, he recommended his countrymen to consume their own manufactures ; not like Berkeley, because he thought it would benefit the Irish, but because he hoped it might hurt the English.   But in the famous controversy respecting "Wood's halfpence," he went much farther.   All the arts, legitimate and illegitimate, of the most accomplished political pamphleteer that ever lived were used to inflame the passions of the people against the attempt of the English Government to give them, not anything injurious, not even anything indifferent, but something they were urgently in need of.   Swift, as every one knows, triumphed.   One Lord-Lieutenant had to resign ; another had to yield.   The Government had to put up with a loss of credit.   The country had to put up with the loss of a much-wanted currency. Angry feeling was roused on all sides, and so far as I know, no good was done to any human being. Now, I am far from denying that, in the course he thus took, Swift was partly animated by a disinterested hatred of the monstrous injustice to which Ireland was habitually subjected by England. What I wish to point out is that, while he belongs to the large class of Irish politicians whose chief public motive is a desire to avenge the wrongs of their country, Berkeley belongs to the very small class whose first desire is to remedy her woes.

Their respective claims on the general gratitude were acknowledged as might have been expected. Berkeley, who in single-minded sincerity had pointed out the true course of national improvement, lived unknown and died unlamented by the mass of his countrymen; even in his own neighbourhood and among his own people, the memory of him did not long survive his departure. Swift pursued a different course and underwent a different fate. If he did not love the people among whom he was compelled to live, at least he hated their enemies. Though he did nothing to mitigate their sufferings, he embodied and

gave effect to their passions. Therefore he became
the idol of the mob. Their pathetic fidelity never
wavered through his years of inaction, sickness, and
idiocy. His death was an occasion of public mourning,
and his memory still lives as that of one of Ireland's
greatest patriots.

Soon after Berkeley had published the last instal-
ment of the *Querist*, his thoughts were drawn from
the general and chronic miseries of the country to the
acute calamities of his own district. The terrible
winter of 1739-40 was followed by famine, the famine
was followed by disease, and Berkeley's mind was
actively turned towards the discovery of expedients
for mitigating both these evils. It so happened that
his American experience had made him acquainted
with *tar water*, *i.e.* water containing the soluble
constituents of tar. With characteristic enthusiasm
he now took up the idea that this simple medicine
was, if not a cure, at least a palliation for most of the
physical ills to which flesh is heir. He dosed himself,
his children, and his neighbours with it. He inves-
tigated the best method of making and administering
it. He induced his friend Prior to assist in advertis-
ing its merits; and he recommended it to the world

in the most singular treatise which has probably ever
proceeded from the pen of an Anglican divine. *Siris*,
as it is called, was written when its author was
occupied half in treating his sick, and half in the lofty,
but somewhat vague speculations dear to him in his
later years. The book accordingly takes its whole
character from these strangely-assorted sources of
inspiration. It begins by enumerating the diseases
for which tar water may be successfully prescribed ;
and few inventors of quack remedies, I should
imagine, have presumed further upon the public
credulity than did Berkeley, in all good faith, when
he published this imposing catalogue. Consumption,
erysipelas, ulcers, dropsy, asthma, pleurisy, gout,
fevers, small-pox, and *all* inflammations, are some of
the maladies which this panacea was expected to cure.
Little more than a third of the treatise, however, is
devoted to this wondrous drug. By a rapid transi-
tion at the end of the 119th section, Berkeley leaves
tar water and plunges into chemistry; from chemistry
he ascends easily to physics ; from physics to metaphysics ; from metaphysics to theology ; so that when
the astonished reader reaches the end of the book he
finds that he has, step by step, been led from the

purely utilitarian, if not vulgar, topics with which it
began, to the airiest heights of mystical philosophy.

The destiny of *Siris* has been as remarkable as are
its contents.   It had an immediate success far exceed-
ing that of any other of its author's works.   Horace
Walpole wrote about this time: "We are now mad
about the water, on the publication of a book written
by Dr. Berkeley, Bishop of Cloyne.   The book
contains every subject from tar water to the Trinity;
however, all the women read it and understand it no
more than if it were intelligible.   A man came into
an apothecary's shop the other day: 'Do you sell
tar water?'   'Tar water?' replied the apothecary,
'why, I sell nothing else!'"   Three editions were
called for in the year of its publication; two more
soon followed.   It was translated into French and
into German.   The remedy it recommended became
the fashion, and the doctors trembled for their
monopoly.   Since then, times have changed.   Tar
water, so suddenly elevated to the dignity of a
universal medicine, has again sunk to the position of
the humblest drug in the Pharmacopeia.   But the
philosophy of the book, which before was only
rendered palatable by its medicine, has now found

admirers for its own sake. In the speculations of
Siris, later thinkers have seen not only a development
of its author's early philosophy, but an anticipation of
systems which have not even yet received their final
expression. As in his youthful writings Berkeley is
the teacher of Hume, so in those of his declining
years he is regarded as the forerunner of the
speculative movement of which a reaction against
Hume was the most notable cause. Without discussing this question at length, I may say that while the
actual value of these metaphysical fragments have, in
my judgment, been exaggerated, their biographical
interest is very great. They show a remarkable
development in the philosopher, though not a development which has been of much value to philosophy.
Berkeley's early work is distinguished not only by
the admirable qualities of originality, lucidity, and
subtlety, but by a less excellent characteristic, which
I can only describe as a certain *thinness* of treatment.
At the time when he produced these immortal
speculations he had read little, and felt little. No
experience of the weary entanglement of concrete
facts had yet suggested to him that a perfect solution
of the problem of the universe is beyond our reach.

He easily exaggerated, therefore, the scope of his discovery, and his youthful self-confidence found no difficulty in believing that, by a simple correction in our theory of perception, all puzzles would be unravelled and all mysteries made plain. Very different was his attitude of mind when, richer by thirty years of experience and study, he gave to the world the fragments of his later Philosophy; and the difference is perceptible on the most cursory comparison of his works at the two dates. In the *Principles of Human Knowledge* its author found little occasion to mention previous systems, except to express his dissent from them. In *Siris* the appeal to authority is so persistent as sometimes to become almost wearisome. In the *Three Dialogues* he designs, so he informs us, "plainly to demonstrate the reality and perfection of human knowledge." In *Siris* he tells us that "with respect to the universe of things we, in this mortal state, are like men educated in Plato's cave," and that "we must be satisfied to make the best of those glimpses within our reach." The earlier works are remarkable for the easy confidence of their reasoning, the clearness and definiteness of their conclusions. In *Siris* there is little that deserves the name of argument, and its teaching is mystic and ill-defined. It is as if by the same intellectual light, which in his youth he had concentrated with such admirable results on a restricted area, he strove, in his later years, to explore the vast and shadowy spaces in which the sages of the ancient world had vainly sought for Absolute Truth, but found that the rays which formerly yielded such definite images now showed only in faint and doubtful outline the eternal framework on which, as Berkeley thought, is reared the fleeting world of sense.

It is rather, therefore, the spirit in which *Siris* is written, than its direct teaching, which appeals to the sympathy of the modern reader. Its fragmentary character, its uncritical wealth of erudition, the crudeness of its science, and the incompleteness of its philosophy, are easily forgiven, on account of its suggestiveness, the large toleration it displays towards widely-different modes of thought, and a certain quality of moral elevation and speculative diffidence alien both to the literature and the life of the eighteenth century. The whole book is, in truth, an anachronism. It draws its inspiration sometimes from the Neo-platonists, sometimes, even, from the alchemists, while sometimes it foreshadows meta-physical systems still in process of formation. But if its mystical speculations were not in harmony with an age taught by Voltaire and Hume, neither were such reflections as the following likely to suit the taste of a nation governed by Walpole or Newcastle :—

Whatever the world thinks, he who hath not much meditated upon God, the human soul, and the *summum bonum*, may possibly make a thriving earthworm, but will most indubitably make a sorry patriot and a sorry statesman.

By utterances such as these Berkeley spiritually severed himself from a generation not much given to meditation—at least in his fashion—either upon God, the soul, or the *summum bonum*. But his work in it was nearly done. The last years at Cloyne were overshadowed by increasing infirmities and domestic losses. Less and less able for business, anxious only for repose, he turned again to his early dream of a life spent in academic retirement. Though it does not appear that he had Oxford friends, he had seen Oxford many years before, and the external aspect of the place (in 1752 much the best part of it) had lingered in his memory as that of a spot where such a dream might well be fulfilled. Thither, accordingly, he removed. The change of air seemed at first to benefit him. He was able to superintend the republication of some of his earlier works, and was in better health than he had been for some years. But the end came suddenly. On the 14th of January 1753, in the midst of his family, without warning and without pain, he passed away : leaving behind him writings which will perpetuate his fame as one of the most admirable of English philosophers, and the memory of a character not, I think, to be surpassed in individuality, or in charm, by any recorded in the history of English men of letters.

III

HANDEL[1]

In the year 1784 was celebrated in Westminster Abbey, with a pomp and circumstance hitherto unknown in musical history, a festival in honour of the centenary of Handel's birth. He had then been laid a quarter of a century among the poets and heroes of his adopted country. His memory was still fresh among us. Many were living who had seen and known him, who had heard him at the organ conducting his oratorios, and who kept alive, amid a younger generation of musicians, the traditions of his style and the recollections of his fame. No great figure had in the meanwhile risen to fill the space left empty in the English world of music by his death. It is true that a musical revolution was in progress,

[1] *Edinburgh Review*, January 1887.

that old things were passing away, and that the first
promise of new artistic developments, undreamed of
in the first half of the eighteenth century, might be
detected by discerning eyes. But it was the first
promise only. In 1784 Haydn had not visited
England, nor, indeed, produced his most considerable
works outside the limits of chamber music. Mozart
was known here chiefly as a youthful prodigy; the
sun of Beethoven had not yet risen above the horizon;
Bach, who had never been known in England, was for
a space forgotten even in Germany; and Handel's
music represented to the majority of our countrymen
the culminating point to which the art had as yet
reached or could, perhaps, be expected to attain.

Since that day a hundred years and more have
passed, years fertile in masterpieces of musical creation. Fashions have changed; tastes have altered.
In music, not less than in poetry and painting, each
generation desires to have, and insists on having, that
which best suits its moods,—which most effectually
appeals to the special quality of its emotions: and
this universal principle of change, which makes it
necessary that the artistic productions of every age,
be they better or be they worse, shall at least be

different from those of the preceding one, has been in the case of music supplemented by other causes which have made the process of alteration one not of change merely, but also of growth. For music alone among her sister arts has profited by the material development of society and the progress of mechanical invention; music alone has been able in any important respect to multiply the methods by which she moves the imagination of mankind. In poetry and in painting, the work of every age and of every man of genius will doubtless be distinguished by its characteristic note. Yet, however differently used, the artistic resources of a poet or a painter to-day are not materially greater than those which a poet or a painter of the sixteenth or seventeenth century had at his command. We cannot flatter ourselves that we know more of colouring than Titian, or of versification than Milton. We could not teach drawing to Michael Angelo, nor rhythm to Shakespeare. In music the case is otherwise. Since the death of Handel there has not only been a remarkable development of musical form, an increased freedom in the use of harmonic resources, and a prodigious growth both in the art of instrumentation and in the

I

variety of instruments, but the modern musician has at his command far better players, far larger orchestras, and far more powerful choirs, than his predecessors ; so that the pettiest composer of the year eighteen hundred and eighty-six is able to produce effects of which Handel and Bach never dreamed, and may employ methods of which they were utterly ignorant.

Thus it comes about that we are divided from the great musical creations of bygone times by more than the inevitable veil which, talk as we may of the immortality of genius, does always somewhat alter, and must, in some cases, dim our perception of the artistic work of the generations which have preceded us. Whatever be the language in which these may speak, whether that of poetry, of painting, or of music, their voices come to us across the centuries with something, be it ever so little, of a foreign accent. But in the case of music, their language has not merely a somewhat unfamiliar turn, it is in certain important respects imperfectly developed ; and the ideas it expresses are necessarily limited with its limitations. So it comes about that the man of average musical cultivation is incomparably more dependent on modern productions than the man of average literary cultivation. Go back a century and a quarter, and take the year 1760, the one which followed Handel's death : how poverty-stricken would our libraries be if all the literary works of imagination which appeared before that date were suddenly destroyed,—if our earliest playwright was Sheridan our earliest poet Goldsmith, our earliest master of prose Dr. Johnson ! It is not merely the student who would suffer by such a catastrophe, the whole educated world would lose an important fraction of its daily literary food. But with music the case is otherwise. The largest portion of the works of even the great musicians before the date I have named have either perished beyond hope of recovery, or slumber in their original manuscript undisturbed on the shelves of our libraries and museums. And it would, I think, be rash to say that, with the exception of Handel and Bach, there is a single composer whose most important works are the familiar companions of the ordinary musical amateur. Now, therefore, that we have just celebrated the bi-centenary of Handel's birth with more than the magnificence which distinguished the celebration of the centenary,

it is a fitting time to ask how far the musical experience of the century,—which is thus, as I have shown,
relatively of far greater importance than a similar
experience in the case of letters or painting,—has
modified the verdict which our great-grandfathers
passed on their adopted countrymen. It is worth
inquiring what is the amount of our debt to him;
what it is that he did which none had done before
him; and how far what he has done has been better
done by those who have come after.

Before going into this question, it may be worth
while to remind the reader of the principal dates in
Handel's artistic career.

Handel, born in 1685, in Lower Saxony, was the
son of a doctor already past middle life. The father
knew nothing, and cared nothing, for music. The
child showed that early and inevitable inclination
towards it which has distinguished so many great
composers. He was designed for the law, but in the
conflict which ensued between the plans of the father
and the tastes of the son, the latter finally prevailed,
and the young Handel commenced his musical education at the age of seven, under Zachau, organist of
Halle Cathedral. Here he acquired all that was to

be learned in the great Organ School, and there was even a moment when he appears to have contemplated taking an organist's place at Lübeck, in which case Bach might have had a rival on his own ground. According to the story, he was prepared to accept all the conditions attaching to the post except that of marrying his predecessor's daughter; and, if this anecdote be true, it is perhaps owing to the absence of charm in this young lady that he has left us opera and oratorio instead of organ music and mass.

As events actually turned out, Italy (which he visited after an important stay at Hamburg) was destined to have nearly as large a share in the formation of his style as Germany. He visited it in 1706; was received with open arms in Rome, Naples, and Venice; made acquaintance with Corelli and A. Scarlatti; composed two oratorios and two operas; and learned all that was taught in what was still the great centre of art education in Europe.

Strong in this combination of Italian and German art, Handel came to England in 1710, and a few weeks afterwards produced the opera "Rinaldo," which has never been surpassed, either by its author or any one else, in the particular style of opera

composition which prevailed in the first half of the
eighteenth century.

A composer of operas he remained in the main for
more than twenty-five years, but he early showed his
genius for that peculiar form of art in which he has
never been excelled, *i.e.* writing for chorus. The
Utrecht and other Te Deums, the Utrecht Jubilate
(1713), the Chandos Anthems (1718), Esther (1719),
and Acis and Galatea (1720), contain the promise, and
more than the promise, of what he was destined
ultimately to accomplish. These last works were
composed while Handel was acting as chapel-master
to the Duke of Chandos. It is interesting, by the
way, to note the extraordinary liberality with which
musical artists, especially in England, were treated in
the earlier part of the last century. Handel received
in pensions from the Crown no less a sum than £500
a year. For the composition of "Esther" he received
£2000. Buononcini, in like manner, is said to have
received a present of £5000 and a pension of £500
from Henrietta, Duchess of Marlborough. Eighty
years later, Beethoven, the spoiled darling of the
Austrian aristocracy, received, at the height of his
fame, a pension of about £140, and £50 for the

greatest of his works. The fact is not less striking if we compare the treatment received respectively by men of letters during the same period and by musicians. In Handel's time, as we all know, literature, not less than art, depended as much on the patronage of the great as on the favour of the public; yet I cannot recall any instance in which a man of letters, however distinguished, received either from the Crown, or from the nobility, anything at all approaching the sums which were lavished upon Handel, and upon Buononcini.

In 1720 was started a Society destined profoundly to affect the future of Handel's career. The Royal Academy of Music was founded in order to promote, on the most magnificent scale, the performances of Italian opera. Handel was appointed its conductor; Buononcini and Ariosti aided him in the work of composition. For some time matters went smoothly enough; but the jealousies which arose between the Society and its conductor, between the rival composers, and between the rival singers, soon produced a degree of discord fatal to that unity of action without which continuous success was impossible. Handel broke with the Society, and set up, first in

1729, in partnership with Heidegger; afterwards (in 1734) on his own account. The results of such a proceeding are what might easily have been antici- pated. Few have been the places, and brief the periods, in which the opera has been able to support itself on any considerable scale in entire independence either of private munificence or State subvention. London, as readers of Colley Cibber's *Apology* are aware, could with difficulty in the early part of the last century support two playhouses. A scheme, therefore, which required that it should support two opera-houses was foredoomed from the first to dis- astrous failure. It did not require the unprecedented success of the "Beggars' Opera" to destroy its exotic rival; that rival was predestined to destruction, had Gay never written, nor Pepusch composed. Handel became bankrupt in 1737, and in the same year was struck down by paralysis. Health and fortune alike deserted him, and so low had he sunk that to rise again might have seemed impossible. But, in truth, what appeared to be the end of his career was, so far as posterity is concerned, almost the beginning of it. He had before this period composed at intervals three oratorios, besides "Acis and Galatea," and

"Alexander's Feast." To oratorio he now almost exclusively devoted himself. In the fourteen years succeeding his bankruptcy he produced the whole of that immortal series (with the exception of "Esther," "Deborah," and "Athaliah") by which his name is for ever rendered illustrious. And although he did little in the way of original compositions after he was attacked by cataract in 1752, his musical activity never ceased. He continued, amid growing fame and increasing prosperity, to conduct his oratorios until the very end. The end came in 1759, only a week after he attended a performance of the "Messiah." He died on the day before Easter Sunday at his house in Brook Street, at the age of seventy-four.

So lived and so died this great artist. That his life was one of ceaseless production,—that he contributed, more than any musician of his time, to the delight of his generation,—is praise that will be grudged him by none. But what is impartial criticism to say of his work in its larger aspects? How far did he improve upon the art of his predecessors? How far did he smooth the path of progress for those who were to come after him? Has he, for an age familiar with the masterpieces of Beethoven,

Mendelssohn, Schumann, and Wagner, any but an
historic interest?

In answer to these questions it must, I think, be
admitted, in the first place, that he cannot be said to
have aided the advance of music in the same degree, or
even in the same sense, as some other of the great
composers I have named.   We can assert with confidence that without Haydn we should not have the
Mozart we know; that without Mozart we should
not have the Beethoven we know; and that without
Beethoven the whole musical history of the nineteenth
century would have been utterly different from what
it is.   No such proposition can be advanced respecting
Handel.   In England, he left behind him some
humble imitators, who were more successful in stealing his phrases than in catching his inspiration, but
he left no school.   On the Continent he did even
less.   His works form, as it were, a monument,
solitary and colossal, raised at the end of some blind
avenue from which the true path of advance has
already branched; a monument which, stately and
splendid though it be, is not the vestibule through
which art has passed to the discovery and exploration
of new regions of beauty.

Intimately connected with this peculiarity is another, deserving of notice in the same connection. Handel was not, as regards the technical method of producing musical effects, in any sense a great innovator; as regards form, he rather exhausted the possibilities of those already in use than added to their number. Consider, for example, his overtures. Delightful and spirited as these are, admirably as they are contrived—not, indeed, like modern overtures, to give a kind of foretaste of the drama which is to follow, but—to attune the minds of the audience to its opening scenes, they are, with rare exceptions, framed on one unvarying model. For more than fifty years he was content to preface opera and oratorio alike with the kind of introduction that was in fashion when, as a youth of nineteen, he wrote his first opera at Hamburg; and the overtures to the "Messiah" and to "Samson," however in other respects superior, did not differ in form from those with which, two generations previously, Lulli had delighted the Court of Louis XIV.

Similar observations may be made respecting his operas. They were, no doubt, by very much the best works of their kind which had ever been pro-

duced. Many of the airs which they contain are
still familiar to us; many more deserve to be so.;
and, even when divorced from their dramatic setting,
may continue to give exquisite delight. But on the
whole it would, I suppose, be true to say that after
expending for more than thirty years his time, his
money, his health, and his unequalled genius, on the
cultivation of the Italian opera, he left it richer,
indeed, by innumerable masterpieces, but in other
respects very much where he found it—fettered,
that is, by endless conditions, imposed not so much
to satisfy the requirements of dramatic propriety as
to moderate the rivalries of competing singers.

It seems at first sight strange that any man of
genius should have patiently submitted to rules
which, from the point of view of art, were perfectly
arbitrary. The explanation is, no doubt, to be found
in the circumstance that up to the middle of the
eighteenth century (speaking very roughly) the
orchestra was a mere adjunct to the voice, and that
the revolution, which seems in these later times to
have made the voice a mere adjunct to the orchestra,
had not even begun. The modern composer for the
stage sometimes writes as if singers were a necessary

evil which have, no doubt, to be endured in order to carry on the dramatic dialogue, but which need to be treated with no sort of consideration. If this be a fault in one direction, a point on which I offer no opinion, the early composers of Italian opera fell, or were driven, into the opposite one. They lived at a time when the powers of execution possessed by performers on every instrument (except, it is said, the trumpet) were very inferior to those which are now common, but when the voice was cultivated with an assiduity and a success which have never since been rivalled. The composers could thus command inimitable technical skill in their singers; but the singers required in their turn a degree and a kind of consideration which has never before or since been asked or received by the interpreters of a work of genius from its creator.

Thus Handel, in most of his operas, not only observed the elaborate system of rules which were contrived to ensure that, while each singer should have sufficient scope to display his talent, no singer should have too much, but wrote his music with a special view to the particular aptitudes of the various members of his staff. It is, I believe, possible to discover, by a mere examination of his score, not only what was the compass of each performer, but what was his peculiar excellence or weakness, and in what part of the register lay his best and most effective notes. We are told that when Cuzzoni and Faustina were performing together at his theatre,— when all London was divided as to their merit: when the strife so engendered rose to a pitch of bitterness which, even in the age of Walpole and Pulteney, surpassed the rage of political parties,—the composer so nicely balanced the *rôles* of the competing singers, contrived with so much skill to give to each exactly equal opportunities for display, and, even when he caused them to sing together in a duet, managed to provide them with parts so precisely alike in prominence and interest, that even the jealousy of rival artists and rival women could not accuse him of partiality. But however much we may admire the ease with which art so trammelled could move, we can no longer be seduced by the voice of a Farinelli or a Faustina into forgetting that the trammels are there. Therefore it is that the Italian opera of Handel's time is dead beyond all hope of revival, even in this age of revivals. No modern audience would tolerate it, even if modern singers could be found to render it; and this, be it observed, not because the music is old-fashioned, not because our ears are tuned to richer orchestration or a different flow of melody, though these things be true, but because the composers of that day were compelled by the tyranny of circumstances to cast their thoughts in a shape which even a genius like Handel's could not render immortal.

For this it would be unfair to blame the composer. The greatest works which the world has seen have not been dedicated to an unknown posterity, but have been produced to satisfy the daily needs of their age, and have, therefore, of necessity conformed to the tastes, and usually to the fashion and the prejudices, of the period which gave them birth. So it was with Handel's operas; and, without doubt, but for two accidental circumstances, it is to the production of operas that he would have mainly devoted himself, to the infinite loss of posterity, even to the very end of his career. These two circumstances were — the rivalries and quarrels already adverted to, which made it impossible profitably to perform operas, — and the observance

of Lent, which made it possible profitably to perform oratorios.   The debt which all the arts owe to
the Church is infinite ; but, perhaps, the heaviest
liabilities have been incurred by music.   It was the
liturgies of the Church which supplied the inspiration
of all the greatest compositions down to comparatively
recent times ; it was Church choirs which supplied
the musical training ; it was Church funds which supplied the necessary endowments.   Slight, indeed, would
be our musical heritage if all was subtracted from it
which had been written for the Church, or by those whom
the Church had helped to teach or to support.   These
benefits to art were due to the *positive* action of the
Church.   That Handel devoted himself exclusively
in his later years to oratorio is due to its *negative*
action.   During Lent, operas were discontinued, and
it was mainly through the accidental advantage thus
given to oratorio in the "struggle for existence," that
they were able to contend successfully against their
more showy rivals.   We owe, therefore, "Israel in
Egypt," the "Messiah," "Semele," and "Hercules,"
to liturgical observance less directly, but not less
really, than the "Missa Papæ Marcelli," the "Passion,
according to St. Matthew," or the "Mass in D."

Judging by the light of posthumous criticism, it may seem strange that Handel should not have left the opera till the opera had to all intents and purposes left him, and that he did not devote himself to oratorio till his theatrical speculations had finally broken down. It is no doubt true that nowhere in Europe had the experiment of oratorio, *i.e.* of dramatic pieces without dramatic action, been tried as a popular entertainment; that it would have been folly to have embarked on such a speculation without full assurance of its success; and that Handel seems to have embarked on it as soon as, by repeated experiment, he was convinced that such assurance had been obtained. But it must be acknowledged that he was not easily convinced. Note the stages through which these experiments passed. "Esther," the first English oratorio, was written for a private patron, and for private performance. "Acis" had the same origin about the same time. Both were written at a period when there was no Italian opera in London, and when therefore, Handel had no other outlet for his dramatic talents. For more than ten years after this the composer, entirely occupied with operas, neither added to the number of his oratorios, nor caused those which he

K

had already finished to be performed. And even then, though sinking to the lowest ebb of fortune, it was due to external influences rather than to his own spontaneous impulse that he began slowly and cautiously to turn his creative energies in what now seems to us their natural direction. The first incidents which led to this were some private performances of "Esther" by the children of the Chapel Royal, *with action and scenery*. This led to a desire for a representation of the same oratorio, by the same performers and in the same way, at the Opera House. But here, fortunately, the Bishop of London stepped in. He was ready to allow the children of the chapel to sing, but not to act. In so doing, he no doubt conceived himself to be furthering the interests of propriety, if not of morality; but he was, in reality, furthering with far more decisive effect the interests of art. It is not wholly impossible that, but for his intervention, Handel would have aimed at the production of a form of oratorio which, in accordance with tradition, would differ little from opera, except in the choice of subject, the somewhat greater freedom of construction, and in the greater prominence given to chorus. In so doing he would, as I shall presently show, have forfeited his deep claim to our gratitude as a musical innovator. His later works would have borne to his earlier very much the same relation that Racine's "Athalie" bears to his "Iphigenie." They would have been more edifying, but not in any artistic quality essentially different or superior. How slowly Handel reconciled himself to the idea of oratorio, as he himself has taught us to understand the term, is further proved, if further proof be wanting, by the fact that the first public performance of "Acis" (not given, it may be noted, until Handel was driven to it in order to forestall an impudent attempt at musical piracy), was represented without action, indeed, but with appropriate scenery, costumes, and decorations. This, however, was a theatrical hybrid that necessarily remained barren. It was a compromise which could not last, and accordingly, in the next year, we see him in "Deborah" and "Athaliah," finally accepting oratorio as a form of entertainment by which he might appeal to the public as he had before appealed to them by opera.

Such were the slow gradations of success by which Handel was, as it were, reluctantly forced to devote the full strength of his matured genius to the exclusive production of that class of works which are for ever connected with his name, and of which he was, perhaps, as much the inventor as, in this world of slow development, any one is the inventor of anything. Antiquarians, it is true, trace the pedigree of the oratorio to the year 1600. They tell us that the first oratorio was composed by Cavaliere, that the name originated in the accidental circumstance that the first performance took place in the oratory of St. Maria, in Vallicella, and they further define this particular form of art for us as a sacred poem, of a dramatic or allegoric character, sung by voices in solo and chorus with orchestral accompaniment.

All this is true, is interesting, and is important. But there is a certain danger that in laying stress on this particular set of historical facts we should forget circumstances not less true, not less interesting, and even more important to the proper comprehension of what was artistically new in Handel's work. In this case, as in others, we have to be careful lest the history of the name should divert our attention from the history of the thing.

Now, what distinguished the oratorio of the early

seventeenth century from the opera of the same date was not the character of the music, but the character of the subject. Both were sung, and both were acted; both consisted of the same succession of airs and recitative, occasionally varied in the same way by slight choruses. The difference between them lay in the fact that the theme of one was sacred, that of the other secular, and it consisted in this fact alone. But this is not a circumstance of the slightest interest, artistically speaking, nor does it in the slightest degree indicate the real difference between Handel's English oratorios and his Italian operas. If any one entertains a doubt on the point let him consider in what categories he would respectively place Handel's Italian work, " Resurrezione," and " Hercules." The first is indistinguishable in form from " Rinaldo "; the second is indistinguishable in form from " Samson." But the first is sacred, the second is secular. The first, therefore, would, and the second would not, be usually called an oratorio. I venture to think that this terminology, however much in accordance with usage, lays stress upon the wrong set of facts. It draws attention to the subject of the words, not to the character of the music,—to the theme selected by the librettist, and not to its treatment by the composer. Now, whether we think it worth while to depart from the ordinary usage of words or not, we shall do well to bear in mind that while the oratorio was, no doubt, in its inception essentially sacred, secular dramas have been successfully treated after the manner of oratorios; and that while the first oratorios were intended to be acted, the vital characteristic of the perfected oratorio is that it is neither acted, nor is, indeed, in most cases, by any possibility capable of being acted.

A little consideration will show that this peculiarity is all-important. Of the three possible ways in which a written drama can be presented to an audience,—namely, as a play, as an opera, or as an oratorio,—the opera has, and in Handel's time had to a much greater extent than now, characteristic weaknesses from which the others are free. In its attempt to re-enforce the emotions produced by acting, through the aid of those produced by music, both the acting and the music suffer. For the whole *raison d'être* of acting is that it sufficiently resembles nature to produce, with the aid of a little good-will on the part of the spectators, a sense of reality. It

is this sense of reality, and this alone, which makes
an acted play more effective than a recited one.   But
if the actors, instead of rendering the emotions of the
characters they represent, are occupied mainly in
rendering the music of the composer,—if they have
to carry on their ordinary conversations in recitative,
and mark the critical situations by the delivery of an
aria,—illusion becomes impossible.   Even the most
perfect acting and the most realistic scenery require
some allowances, and can only be accepted by the aid
of certain tacit conventions ; but it is too great a
strain to put upon our powers of self-deception to ask
us to accept as true to nature ladies and gentlemen
who make love in elaborate duets or die in the
execution of a trill.   No doubt, in recent times a
successful effort has been made to diminish these
objections by throwing the chief musical interest into
the orchestra, and by altogether preventing the performers from stopping the action of the drama by the
execution of set pieces of music ; but in Handel's age
such a device would have been impossible, if for no
other reason yet because the orchestra of those times
was utterly unfit to bear the weight of so heavy a
responsibility.

If in opera the music impaired the verisimilitude of the acting, it is not less true that acting limited the variety of the music. Before the instrumental revolution of the last hundred and fifty years, the most powerful musical effects, without comparison, which the musician could command were produced by the chorus; and the use of choruses was strictly limited both by dramatic convention and by stage necessities. So that in Handel's case we have the extraordinary absurdity of the greatest master of choral effect the world has ever seen restricted to the composition of recitatives and airs, only here and there relieved by the meagre and trifling choruses permitted by the rules and practice of the Italian opera.

In giving up the attempt to combine dramatic music with dramatic representation, the oratorio freed itself at once from all these absurdities, and all these limitations. It ceased to be acting marred by singing; it became recitation glorified by music; and this gave it another advantage, of which it is necessary to take note. The story of a drama written for the stage, or framed on the model of those that are so written, is necessarily given in the words of the various *dramatis personæ*; in this respect differing from a piece written in the epic, narrative, or descriptive form. But this difference, vital as it is when we are dealing with plays or poems, loses all importance in the case of oratorios. It is superfluous to distinguish an oratorio like "Samson," in which everything is sung by personages in the story,—Delilah, Manoah, Israelitish women, and so forth,—from one like "Israel in Egypt," in which there are no personages at all, but only a series of descriptions. You may, if you please, call one dramatic and the other epic, but the distinction is here immaterial. Both consist essentially of a connected series of incidents stated in words, and interpreted by music. And provided the incidents be of a kind which lend themselves to such interpretation,—provided they be sufficiently connected to give unity, sufficiently contrasted to give variety, and at the same time fairly co-ordinated into an artistic whole,—the librettist need trouble himself no more about the possibilities of stage representation than he need about the unities of time and place.

But the superiority of the oratorio over its dramatic rival as an "art form" is not more decisive than its superiority over its Church rivals, the Passion

and the Mass. We must not be misled in this matter
by the splendour of the music associated with these
names ; for it is not the music I am discussing, but
the use to which the music has been put; the
"poetic form" to which it has been wedded. Now
the libretto of a Passion music was simply a Mediæval
miracle play born out of due season. It had all the
limitations which arise from the fact that it dealt
with only one subject in only one way, added to all
the limitations due to the circumstance that its
object was not æsthetic, but devotional,—that it was
intended to promote, not pleasure, but edification.
It is impossible but that the music with which it was
associated should suffer from these disadvantages ;
that it has so suffered may be inferred from the fact
that it has been (comparatively speaking) seldom set
by musicians of genius, that of all the sittings there
is but one in which posterity takes much interest,
and that to do full justice to this one we have to
remember that it must be judged from the point of
view of a religious ceremony in which the audience
were expected to take a part.

Observations not wholly dissimilar may be made
respecting the Mass as a theme for musical treatment.

If intended for use in church it can only be regarded as an accessory to the most solemn act of Christian worship, and must necessarily be interrupted by those parts of the service which are not sung by the choir. If intended for the concert-room it can only be considered as a sacred cantata on a somewhat extended scale, of which the succession of ideas, however consecrated by usage, has been determined by liturgical and not by artistic considerations.

The oratorio, then, stands pre-eminent, at least in the infancy of orchestration, among all the modes in which music may be wedded to dramatic poetry. It, and it alone, gives the musician the utmost latitude in the choice of his subject, and in the employment of his resources. It is Handel's glory to have perceived its capabilities, and to have developed them in a manner undreamed of by his predecessors, and unsurpassed by even the greatest of his successors. He brought to this task a peculiar combination of gifts. His long connection with the operatic stage had brought to perfection the dramatic genius and the inexhaustible flow of melody which he inherited from Nature. He was able to combine this with a power of choral composition already exercised in the

great series of "Chandos Anthems," in the various
settings of the "Te Deum," and in other compositions
for the Church, and which, in its kind, has never
since been approached. All that was great in opera,
all that was great in Church music, together with
much that stage limitations excluded from the first,
and religious feeling from the second, thus united to
adorn dramatic narratives, which, however indifferent
as literature, were seldom deficient in powerful situations well fitted for musical treatment.[1]

It is not necessary here to dwell at length on the
characteristics which, as we are told so often and so
truly, distinguish his style, especially in choruses.

---

[1] Handel has, indeed, been, on the whole, fortunate in the
pieces he has set. Some of them were by the most distinguished
men of letters of his own and the preceding age. Not to mention
the cantatas composed to words by Milton and Dryden, Pope is
said to have written "Esther"; Gay wrote "Acis"; Congreve
wrote "Semele"; "Athaliah" was based on Racine; and the
text of "Samson" is Milton spoiled. From names like these it is
something of a descent to go to Mr. Jennens and Dr. Morell. But
even Mr. Jennens, and Dr. Morell, and a clergyman of the name
of Miller, who surpassed even these in the art of sinking in poetry,
though they were far from being either tolerable versifiers or
tolerable playwrights, knew something of their business. They
supplied a certain number of incidents, described in a certain
quantity of doggrel, wisely leaving it to the composer to furnish
the genius and the imagination. Accordingly, they produced not
unsuccessful librettos, when better men might, perhaps, have only
succeeded in giving us not unsuccessful poems.

The grandeur, the contrapuntal learning, the ingenuity with which that learning is concealed, the melodious smoothness of the part-writing, and the extreme simplicity of the means often employed to produce the most striking effects,—all these are familiar qualities of a familiar composer, on which it would be wearisome to dilate, unless with an amount of technical discussion and illustration wholly out of place in this essay. Yet criticism should have something to say without lapsing into the platitudes of eulogistic commonplace on the one side, or into minute and, to most readers, dry and tedious commentary on the other. It is not, perhaps, very easy to say it, and it is not rendered much easier on this occasion by the fact that the writer of these pages is obliged to confess to a degree of affectionate devotion to the great composer which it is not possible, or I had almost even said, which it is not desirable, that the majority of readers should show. Yet, as it is permissible to feel for living personalities a degree of regard not nicely apportioned to the number and quality of their virtues, as we may have a tenderness even for their shortcomings, a lurking affection even for their very weaknesses, the same latitude of toleration must now and again be granted us in another sphere. In art as well as in life we must sometimes be allowed to feel that the native splendour of what is best in any man's work illumines, though with a borrowed glow, those parts which are less excellent, without being too constantly reminded that the glow is borrowed. In art as well as in life it must be given us sometimes to judge as lovers, and not with the chill impartiality of mere intimate acquaintance.

A sentiment of this kind need not, we may hope, impair the worth of criticism unless the critic is rendered by it incapable of separating what is personal in his estimate, from that which is universal, unless it induces him to try and impose on the world in general the results of his own idiosyncrasies as if they were the products of tastes in which he might expect the rest of mankind to share. From this danger I shall endeavour to guard myself; and, in order that my readers may feel reassured on the point, I hasten to acknowledge that if, as is probable, they are only restrained by the respect inspired by a great name from saying that Handel is not unfrequently simple even to the verge, or beyond the verge, of commonplace, I agree with them, even though to me he is never tame. If they think that Handel was frequently content to use again and yet again phrases originally invented, perhaps, by others, then worn threadbare through constant iteration by himself, I admit it to be true, though to me they seem always fresh. And if they further desire to point out that Handel had certain tricks for producing some of his great choral effects, striking, no doubt, and characteristically simple, but still of a kind from which time and repetition have removed all the novelty and much of the charm, again I agree, though they still charm me.

The truth is that, to every genius there is a characteristic weakness, a defect to which it naturally leans, and into which, in those inevitable moments when inspiration flags, it is apt to subside. With Handel this bias was towards melodious and facile, though always vigorous, commonplace: as with Bach, it was towards a crabbed and somewhat ungrateful treatment of his materials. And in this, as in some other respects, the external circumstances of the two great contemporaries favoured their original differences. Handel wrote to please the public by whom he lived. Engaged, on his own behalf or on that of others, as

the manager of those musical enterprises for which
he was also the composer, he necessarily failed in the
first of these capacities unless he was popular in the
second.   Nor was the public which had to be attracted
either large in numbers or constant in taste.   "The
town," as I have said, could scarcely, at the best,
support two playhouses.   It could not, even with
the aid of enormous private subventions, support two
opera-houses.   And, as the audiences at Drury Lane
deserted Vanbrugh and Congreve for the pantomime,
so the audience at the Haymarket deserted Handel
and Buononcini for the "Beggars' Opera."   Handel,
therefore, is in the same category as the majority of
great creative geniuses.   He was obliged to please
his own age; he might please posterity if he could.
Bach, on the other hand, belongs to the smaller,
and, on the whole, perhaps, not more fortunate class,
whose contemporary public is so limited that, as
regards most of their work, they may almost be said
to have had only themselves to please.   While Handel
was struggling with the administrative difficulties of
the London opera, Bach was organist of Leipsic.
There it was that he produced his greatest works,
and collected round him a devoted and admiring

body of pupils. But from the public he neither desired anything nor got anything. It was his business to compose a certain number of sacred cantatas for the festivals of the Church, and he composed them. It was the business of the worthy burghers of Leipsic to listen to them,—and they listened to them. There is no evidence that the great composer ever sought to excite their enthusiastic appreciation, and there is every evidence to prove that he never obtained it. He laboured at art for art's sake, with all the good, and some, perhaps, of the evil results that not uncommonly attend that operation; and he has had his appropriate reward. He is,—what Handel has never been, nor would ever perhaps have desired to be,—above all things, an artist's artist; one who enjoys chiefly the admiration of experts, but enjoys that in overflowing measure.

There is one other criticism on Handel's work more often explicitly avowed, though not, perhaps, so often felt as those to which I have alluded, which I notice only that I may express my own emphatic dissent from it. We are frequently told that Handel is not original. If by this is meant that he freely used the tags and commonplaces that were the common property of the musicians of his day, or that some of his instrumental slow movements, for instance, show in every note of them unmistakable signs of the influence of Corelli, it is no doubt true, though not very interesting or important. But more than this is usually implied, if it is not actually stated. We are given to understand that his un-acknowledged robberies from contemporaries and predecessors were of a kind and magnitude which must seriously affect our estimate of him, both as an honest man and as an original genius. In support of this indictment, recent investigators have drawn up so formidable a catalogue of these borrowed treasures, that at first sight it would almost appear as if Handel rather compiled music than composed it; and that his works were due not so much to his own natural inspiration as to the assiduous piecing together of the fragments of other men's labours. Now, the actual facts on which this theory rests I take to be these :—After excluding from the list of mis-appropriations those examples in which the resemblance is too shadowy, or the alleged plagiarism [1]

[1] For instance, the alleged imitation in the chorus "Hear,

too improbable to make them adequate foundations
of any judgment adverse to his fame, there undoubtedly remains embedded in his mightiest
creations a large quantity of material borrowed
principally from his own earlier writings, but to no
inconsiderable extent from the writings of other
musicians also. This re-use of old materials is of
the most varying degree of importance. Sometimes
it merely consists in the employment of a fugue
subject which had exercised the ingenuity or stimulated the imagination of composers for the preceding
two hundred years; *e.g.* the series of four ascending
and descending notes which Handel has used in the
"Horse and his Rider," and in the "Hallelujah
Chorus" ("Messiah"), and elsewhere, and which
Byrd, nearly two hundred years previously, set to
the words, "Non nobis Domine." Of this species of
plagiarism, no one, even superficially acquainted with
the practice of musicians in the fifteenth, sixteenth,

Jacob's God" of a chorus by Stradella. I may here take note of
the singular anxiety of critics to discover Handelian plagiarisms.
The excellent article on Handel, for instance, in the *Dictionary
of Music* accuses him of stealing the subject of "Wretched
Lovers" from Bach's forty-eight preludes and fugues. The first
set of the latter was published in 1722, the former was written
in 1720.

seventeenth, and eighteenth centuries, will see anything to wonder at or to criticise. But, again,
sometimes it consists in the working up, perhaps,
into some great chorus, material, his own or borrowed,
which had formerly served a less august and stately
purpose. Interesting examples are to be found in
the use made of the Italian chamber duet in the
chorus "Wretched Lovers"; in the use made of the
ground base to an air in the tenth Chandos Anthem,
in the rolling, oceanic accompaniment of the chorus,
"The waters overwhelmed them" ("Israel"); in the
use made of the theme of the quick movement in
one of the violin sonatas as the subject of the
triumphant choral fugue, "Live, live for ever"
("Solomon"); in the use made of the opening movement of the fourth organ concerto in the accompaniment to a chorus in "Alcina"; and (to turn to
similar adaptations made from other men's works)
of the use made of the introductory phrase in Urio's
"Te Deum" in the chorus, "David his ten thousands
slew" ("Saul"). Again, it may consist in the
appropriation of large fragments of earlier works,
by himself or other people, and their employment
unaltered, or nearly unaltered, as episodes in new

compositions of his own. See, for example, a chorus of Astorga's, embedded as it were in "Then shall they know" ("Samson"); and a chorus by Urio, developed into "Our fainting courage" ("Saul"). Finally, it may consist in the simple transference, with or without an alteration of the words, of a piece of music from one composition to another. Thus he is said to have appropriated the (to say the truth, somewhat dry) chorus, "Egypt was glad" ("Israel"), from an organ-piece by Kerl, without the alteration of a note; and thus he introduced, without modification, into "Deborah," much of the music which had previously done service in the Coronation Anthems, and in the Passion music.

This, then, is an outline of the facts. How are we to interpret them? It will be noted that in the above rude classification I have lumped together, as if they were of the same kind, the robberies which Handel, like Bach, made from himself, and the robberies which he made at the expense of other people. The truth is that, æsthetically and artistically, I do not say morally, they *are* of the same kind. His method of working appears to have been this :— He composed with extraordinary, even preternatural,

rapidity, after relatively long intervals of unpro-
ductive repose. If the dates given in his MSS. are
to be taken as indicating the whole time spent on the
completion of the work, we have to suppose that the
"Messiah," for instance, took only twenty-four days;
"Hercules" only twenty-nine days; "Semele" only
thirty-one days; and "Judas" only thirty-three days,
and so of the others. Doubtless, some time may
in certain cases have been occupied in filling in
the score after the day set down as the final one of
composition; doubtless, also, the work must have
been incubating and maturing long before he put
pen to paper. During this period, and during the
heat and fervour of actual composition, it would
seem that he took his materials where he could find
them, with a serene indifference as to whether they
were old or new, his own or other people's, the work
of a composer long since dead, or the newest growth
of his own inexhaustible genius. Rarely, therefore,
unless in the case of a *pièce d'occasion*, do these
borrowed pieces bear the marks of being foisted into
their places to save the composer trouble, or to
cover a momentary failure of inspiration; in the
great majority of cases (I do not say in all) the

appropriated ideas seem only then to have found the setting and the use for which Nature originally intended them, when Handel impressed them into his service.[1] They are wanderers, which have at last reached their home,—migrating souls, which, not till then, have found their fitting and perfect embodiment.

This, I apprehend, indicates the test which we ought to apply in forming a judgment on the artistic merits of a plagiarism. If the borrowed fragment shows like the marble capitol of a Corinthian column built into the brickwork of a Mediæval wall, the theft is a mistake; and mistakes are crimes,—indeed, the only crimes recognised in the jurisprudence of art. But if it not only fits harmoniously into the new structure, but shows there for the first time its latent capabilities of beauty or of grandeur, then, whatever judgment we may pass on the morality of the plagiarist,

---

[1] So much is this the case that the able, learned, and enthusiastic biographer of Handel, Mr. Rockstro, so well known for his labours in musical history and criticism, actually founds on it a theory that Urio made his "Te Deum" out of fragments of Handel, instead of *vice versâ*. The theory will hardly hold water. That it should ever have been advanced is a proof, if proof be wanting, of the proposition advanced in the text.

the plagiarism, as I conceive, stands justified at
the bar of criticism.   To suppose, indeed, that
the originality of a work like "Israel in Egypt"
is affected by any amount of such plagiarism as
I have described seems to me to ignore the essence
of that in which creative originality consists.   Of
all Handel's works, none perhaps owe less than
the "Messiah," and none owe more than "Israel,"
to the labours of other composers.   Of these two
immortal creations it is hard to say which is the
most perfect.   But there can be no doubt, as I
think, not only that "Israel" is the one most
characteristically Handelian, but that it stands out
amid all creations of the last century, whether of
poets, painters, or musicians, unique in its un-
borrowed majesty.   To suppose that any amount
of laborious grubbing among the scattered MSS.
of forgotten musicians can shake a conclusion like
this, if in other respects it be well founded, is as
rational as to suppose that, by dint of sedulous inquiry, we could mete out the glory of having built St.
Paul's among the quarrymen who provided the
materials.

But, it will be said, the question of morality

still remains. It cannot be right for a great writer to appropriate the work of a small one, and at the same time wrong for a small one to appropriate the work of a great one. Bare justice requires that a common rule should apply to both.

I will not venture on a full discussion of the casuistical problem thus raised. An interesting chapter remains to be written on the history of "private property in thought." When this is accomplished, it will become clear, I believe, that while, at the revival of learning and before it, the unwritten code regulating such matters was so lax that it was by no means considered necessary to acknowledge even direct quotations, the monopoly has become stricter and stricter down to our own time. And it will also be found that some of the greatest and most original geniuses—Shakespeare, for instance, and Molière—have distinguished themselves by the readiness with which they have made use of other men's inventions. Among such is Handel; and with regard to him, and before finally dismissing this topic, I will only make two further observations. The first is, that he does not himself seem to have regarded it as a thing to be ashamed of. Among the most astonishing feats of appropriation which are laid to his charge is the wholesale transference of large fragments of a "Magnificat" by an obscure musician of the name of Erba, to the score of "Israel in Egypt." Now, one of the only two copies of this "Magnificat" known to exist is in Handel's handwriting, and is preserved among his manuscripts at Buckingham Palace. But what is the history of these manuscripts? They are by no means casual chips from his musical workshop, scraped together from holes and corners, and arranged for the first time after his death. On the contrary, Handel himself, always sedulous of his fame, set the greatest store by them. He intended leaving them to his amanuensis, the elder Smith. He quarrelled with Smith and then proposed to leave them to the University of Oxford. He and Smith afterwards became reconciled, and he reverted to his original intentions. If, therefore, we are to believe that in employing Erba's materials he was committing what he considered, or what, in his opinion, others might consider, a breach of morality, we must suppose him to be guilty of the extra-

ordinary folly of leaving the evidence of his mis-
demeanour in a convenient and carefully-preserved
shape among the papers on which he relied for the
honourable perpetuation of his memory. And we
must further suppose that he could venture to
quarrel with a man so intimately acquainted with
all the secrets, and according to the hypothesis,
the discreditable secrets, of his method, as was
Smith ; and that, with the fate of Buononcini before
his eyes, in a country which possessed its share
of learned musicians,[1] and where Handel possessed
more than his share of open enemies and jealous
friends, he was prepared to risk reputation and
livelihood at once in order to save himself a few
hours' extra exertion.

My second observation is this. If the main
objection to robbery consists in the fact that the
victim of the robbery is injured by it, Handel's
appropriation of the music of his predecessors would
seem to be innocent, if not meritorious. So far
from their being injured by it in the quarter in
which injury was alone possible, namely, their

[1] Among the most learned of whom was Pepusch, whom
Handel had ousted at Canons, and who had compiled the
"Beggars' Opera," which ruined Handel's operatic speculations.

reputation, it is not too much to say that their whole reputation is entirely founded on it. Who would take the slightest interest in Urio if Handel had not condescended to use his "Te Deum" in "Saul" and in the "Dottingen"? Who would ever have heard of Erba if Handel had not immortalised him by introducing parts of his "Magnificat" into "Israel"? The truth is that Handel has not cheated them *out of* their due meed of fame, he has cheated them *into* it. And I apprehend that if this were made a preliminary condition of all literary or artistic pilfering, the art of plagiarism would not in all probability be extensively practised or grossly abused.

From this long parenthesis on the nature and extent of Handel's debts to other composers, rendered necessary by the tone and temper, rather perhaps than by the direct assertions of some contemporary criticism, I turn to the more grateful task of dwelling for a moment on the nature and extent of our debts to him. And perhaps, if I had to describe his special and transcendent merit in a few words, I should say that it consisted in his unequalled power of using chorus to express every shade of definite dramatic emotion. And in this connection I do not think sufficient attention has been paid to the astonishing range which Handel attempted to cover in his choral compositions, or to the success which attended his efforts. Other composers, though surely not many, have equalled him in the dramatic treatment of the solo voice. One other man has equalled him in the easy and admirable mastery of choral technique. But no man has equalled him, scarcely any man has tried to equal him, in the free application of chorus to every dramatic purpose, and to the delineation of every human emotion which language is capable of describing. Before his time, and to no small extent since, chorus writing on a grand scale was reserved almost exclusively for the service of the Church. It was used, with scarcely an exception, as the vehicle of devotion and as the handmaid of liturgical observance,—an august and splendid function, but one, from the very nature of the case, circumscribed and limited. No art, indeed, has exhausted, or will ever exhaust, the possibilities of religious feeling. But no art has consented to confine its efforts to the expression of religious feeling alone. Sooner or later, each has sought new worlds to conquer, and, so far as regards music, with which alone we are now concerned, it is to Handel that we owe the most convincing proof that the greatest resources of chorus could find a use outside the limits of Passion music, Anthem, and Mass, in the vast and varied field of secular emotion.

It will perhaps be said that, after all, most of Handel's oratorios are sacred, and that in such works as "Samson," "Solomon," "Joshua," and "Jephtha," whose subject is taken from Bible history, as well as in those like "Theodora," "Alexander Balus," and "Judas Maccabæus," where the story is distinctly "edifying," he has limited himself to the sphere of religion almost as closely as if he had written only for the Church. But this is not so. Even of the "Messiah," it would not be accurate to say that it is religious in the same sense (though doubtless it is so in as true a sense) as the Mass in B minor. A Mass, like all other music that is or may be used for ecclesiastical purposes, is in the main intended to give heightened expression to the religious feelings of the individual believers engaged in a common act of worship. The "Messiah," on the other hand, is a drama, though a drama unique in its kind. While it might be too much to say that worship is absolutely excluded from it, since it incidentally contains, not prayer, indeed, but praise, yet worship is in no sense its object, but, as in the case of other dramas, the presentation of a series of facts, external to the audience, united into an artistic and organic whole. But, though a drama, it is not an historic drama. If it touches, when necessary, on such historical events, as, for instance, the Nativity, it does so only in their most generalised and symbolic form, not as events in a chronological narrative. Its theme is nothing less than the New Dispensation, as understood and accepted by Christendom; and only familiarity, I think, blinds us to the singularity of the subject, and the skill with which it has been treated by librettist and composer (if, indeed, these are, in this case, to be distinguished). The dangers of the subject, artistically speaking, are obvious. The composer, with such a theme to deal with, might have been tempted to set to music a theological system; he might even have had the perversity to make his system controversial, and given, in admirable counterpoint, his special views on justification by faith and baptismal regeneration. Handel

committed no such error.[1] The work is perfect, not
merely in its separate parts, but it is perfect as a
whole.   Everywhere the emotional side proper for
musical treatment has been kept before the hearer ;
and, through the admirable selection of the words,
the theme has not unfrequently risen to heights
where Handel's strength of wing, and his perhaps
alone, has been able to follow it. Few even of the
greatest among poets, musicians, and (since the
Revised Version, we may now add) scholars, have
succeeded in touching the words of our English
Bible without rushing on disaster. That which they
have found strong they have too often left feeble.
That which they have found sublime they have not
seldom left ridiculous. Of Handel, and of Handel

---

[1] Dogma, it may be noted, must necessarily receive musical
exposition in every setting of the Mass : and it is one of the objections to that portion of the liturgy being used as, to all intents
and purposes, a musical libretto. In Mr. Poole's excellent little
Life of Bach he informs us that in the Creed of the B minor Mass
the Union of the Divine and the human nature in Christ is represented by " a canon first in unison then in the fourth below." It
is not impossible. The history of literature and art sufficiently
proves that in the way of conceits nothing is impossible. But if
it be so, the fact is sufficient to show how unfitted the subject is
to be treated musically. We presume that, if Bach had been required to treat musically the doctrines of the Trinity, he would
have done it in a canon, three in one, at the unison.

only can we say that the most splendid inspirations
of Hebrew poetry gain an added glory from his
music, and that thousands exist for whom passages
of Scripture which have for eighteen centuries been
very near the heart of Christendom acquire a yet
deeper meaning, a yet more spiritual power, through
the strains with which his genius has inseparably
associated them.

But if the "Messiah," though undoubtedly a
religious work, is to be thus distinguished artistically
from those great ecclesiastical compositions to which
choral writers had chiefly devoted themselves; still
more widely separated from such are the bulk of
Handel's oratorios, whether their subjects are
borrowed from the Bible or not. It is true that
magnificent religious music is to be found in most of
them ; but it is, on the face of it, introduced in
obedience to the dramatic necessities of the situation,
and is found side by side with music very different
in character, but scarcely less magnificent, devoted
to the praise of Baal, of Dagon, of Moloch, of Sesach,
of Mithra, of Venus, and of other heathen deities
(for Handel's Pantheon was large !), interspersed
with much love-making and even more fighting.

M

The historic causes, I had almost said the historic accidents, to which we owe the great bulk of Handel's choral work not intended for ecclesiastical purposes, have been already explained. But the spontaneous origin of "Esther" and of "Acis" shows that he did not devote himself to unacted choral drama from necessity till he had first tried his hand at it from choice; while we may, perhaps, conjecture, from the solitary and, at the time, unsuccessful experiment of "Israel," that he was prepared to go even farther than he did in the use of chorus had he found a public ready to follow him. To our eternal loss, it was not to be. The sheer grandeur of the unbroken choral series in which Handel described the most thrilling and impressive of national episodes, was too severe a strain upon the patience of a London public in the reign of George II. to be often repeated; and even down to a comparatively recent date it has been found necessary to relieve the audience and spoil the work by the introduction of a few adapted airs.

But we need not forget what we have, in vain speculations as to what under happier circumstances we might possibly have obtained. Let any who desire to form a judgment on this subject run over, as a preliminary exercise, the following list of twenty choruses. I have paired the first eighteen according to similarity of subject, so that different modes of treating like themes may be compared :—(1) "Envy, eldest born of hell" ("Saul"), "Oh, calumny" ("Alexander Balus"). (2) "Hear, Jacob's God" ("Samson"), "Immortal Lord" ("Deborah"). (3) "Oh, Baal" ("Deborah"), "Ye tutelar gods" ("Belshazzar"). (4) "Crown with festal pomp" ("Hercules"), "From the censer" ("Solomon"). (5) "Wanton god of amorous fire" ("Hercules"), "Let no rash intruder" ("Solomon"). (6) "Righteous Heaven beholds their guilt" ("Susannah"), "By slow degrees the wrath of God" ("Belshazzar"). (7) "Tyrants now no more" ("Hercules"), "Mourn, ye afflicted children" ("Judas"). (8) "We never will bow down" ("Judas"), "Ye sons of Israel" ("Joshua"). (9) "Fixed in his everlasting seat" ("Samson"), "When his loud voice" ("Jephtha"). (10) "Draw the tear" ("Solomon"), "He saw the lovely youth" ("Theodora").

Let the reader further recollect that this list excludes the whole body of his compositions for the

Church; that it contains nothing from "Israel," and nothing from the "Messiah"; that such master-pieces of descriptive and dramatic chorus-writing as are contained in "Acis and Galatea," "Alexander's Feast," "St. Cecilia's Day," "Semele," and other oratorios, find no place in it; and he will have convincing proof that variety and originality are as remarkable characteristics of Handel's choral composition as, by common consent, simplicity and grandeur are allowed to be.

Our first impression, perhaps, of the composer's choral style is that, putting aside music of a strictly religious kind, it lends itself most easily to the expression of popular sentiment in all its massive directness. A nation's mourning or a nation's triumph, national thanksgiving, national worship, the din of battle and the song of victory,—these may seem the subjects best suited to the large canvas and the broad touch of the Handelian manner. Yet this would, perhaps, be a rash judgment unless we can show that he fell short of success in dealing with subjects and situations of a different kind. Love, which occupies a large space in Handel's as in all other dramatic narrative, and which is dragged into his Biblical oratorios in a manner which not seldom verges, according to modern ideas, on the ludicrous, naturally falls, as a rule, to be treated by the single voice or in duet. But the three choruses I have already quoted, "Draw the tear from hopeless love," "May no rash intruder," and "Wanton god of amorous fire," absolutely diverse as they are both in sentiment and musical treatment, are a sufficient proof that the writer of "Love in her eyes sits playing," and of "Where e'er you walk," could, when he so desired it, throw as much passion into his choruses as he could into his solos. Again, what could be more perfect than the manner in which the composer of "Israel in Egypt" has caught the pastoral note in "Acis and Galatea"? The task was far from an easy one. With rare exceptions it may be asserted that every poem of the last century, in so far as it is either pastoral or mythological, is certain to be frigid and artificial, and almost certain to be intolerably dull. Gay's poem was both pastoral and mythological. Yet, as treated by Handel, so far is it from being either frigid or dull, that there is not a frigid or a dull thing in it. The unhappy loves of Nymph and

Shepherd are portrayed with a tender sentiment, from which the tragic note is yet carefully excluded. The "Monster Polypheme," grotesque and yet terrible, is not only drawn in both characters with admirable skill, but plays his part as villain of the piece with no undue or discordant emphasis, while the whole drama is acted against a pastoral background, so fresh and delicious, so like the country on a breezy summer-day, and so unlike the country as it was portrayed in the fashionable pastorals of that period, that it is manifestly not from such sources that Handel drew his inspiration.

In extreme contrast to the pastoral charm of "Acis," at the other end of the dramatic scale, we find the composer attempting tasks of not less difficulty with not less success. To take a single example. There is no incident of Biblical, — or, indeed, of any other,—narrative more charged with dramatic meaning than the interruption of Belshazzar's feast by the mystic writing on the wall. But it is not one specially suited for musical treatment, particularly for musical treatment unassisted by action and scenic effect. If the reader will glance at the way Handel has dealt with the problem, keeping in mind that he had to trust entirely to the imagination of his audience to supply the stage properties; that the parts of "Belshazzar the king, his lords, his wives, and his concubines," were taken by gentlemen and ladies in ordinary evening dress; that the Babylonian banqueting-hall was represented by the benches of a concert-room; that the writing, ominous of impending doom, though talked about, could not, from the nature of the case, be represented; keeping in mind, above all, that Handel had it not in his power to help himself out of the difficulty by any of the orchestral devices open to a modern composer; and it will, I think, be felt that his genius has exhausted the utmost possibilities offered by the materials which he had at his command. At the end of the first act the scene opens. The desecration of the sacred vessels taken from the temple at Jerusalem is protested against in a chorus of admirable and solemn dignity, supposed to be sung by captive Jews; and, on Belshazzar's stubborn refusal to yield on this point to their protest or the entreaties of his mother, the stroke of inevitable retribution is foretold in the great chorus, "By slow degrees the wrath of God,"

which closes the act. In the middle of the second act
we are given the sequel of the scene. The wild revel,
vigorously rendered in the chorus " Ye tutelar gods,"
and in the drinking song of Belshazzar, " Let the
deep bowl," reaches its riotous culmination. Then
suddenly is seen the hand tracing on the wall, in
unknown characters, the decree of fate. The horror
of the king, the confusion among the guests, the
instantaneous change from the half-drunken gaiety of
the revellers to a terror the more awful because its
cause is mysterious and supernatural, are rendered in
the chorus of Babylonian courtiers which follows,
with a force not surpassed in simple strength even by
the narrative as it occurs in the Book of Daniel.

I have now said perhaps enough to vindicate the
claim put forward a few pages back on behalf of the
great composer, that the variety and dramatic force
of the effects which he obtained by the use of chorus
are as remarkable and unique as are their simplicity
and grandeur. But let it not be inferred from the
insistence with which I have spoken of his choruses,
either that his airs and recitatives are other than of
supreme excellence or that his choruses can be with
advantage considered as independent and isolated

compositions, apart from the setting in which Handel originally placed them. The truth is that no musician who has ever lived,—not Mozart nor Schubert,—has been endowed by nature with a more copious, fluent, and delightful gift of melody than he. The aria, indeed, suffers more quickly from the touch of Time than the less fragile structure of chorus or symphony. It wears less well, in part, no doubt, because it was in many cases originally written as much to display the agility of the singer as the genius of the composer. Yet, make what abatement we choose from the enduring merit of Handel's compositions for the solo voice, either on account of their old-fashioned and somewhat formal arrangement into a *first* part, a *second* part, and a *da capo*; or on account of the well-worn "divisions" and turns of phrase, characteristic, indeed, of the age, but most of all characteristic of a composer who, with all his originality, never sought for a new device when an old one would serve his purpose; enough will still remain to justify us in ranking him among the very greatest masters of song that the world has seen. In his airs and accompanied recitatives, in spite of a manner which here and there verges on mannerism, how he plays at will over the whole gamut of human passion! From triumph to despair, from love to frantic fury and desperation, for whatever purpose it may be required, his power of using melody with dramatic force is rarely found wanting.

One quality of emotion, and, as I think, one only, is but faintly and imperfectly represented in his writings; though, unfortunately, perhaps, for his fame, it is the one most valued in modern art. To describe this with accuracy, nay, to describe it at all, is scarcely possible. Even to indicate vaguely its nature is not easy; since music, not literature, has been its chief exponent, and for these fine shades of sentiment language scarcely provides a terminology of sufficient delicacy and precision. Pathos hardly renders it; for though it can hardly be cheerful, it need be impregnated with no more than the faintest and most luxurious flavour of melancholy. There is in it something indirect, ambiguous, complex. Though in itself positive enough, it is, perhaps, most easily described by negatives. It is not grief, nor joy, nor despair, nor merriment. It is no simple emotion struck direct out of the heart by the shock of some great calamity or some unlooked-for good

fortune. If it suggests, as it often does, an un-
satisfied longing, it is a longing vague and far off
which reaches towards no defined or concrete object.
It is the product and the delight of a highly-wrought
civilisation, but of a civilisation restless and tormented,
neither contented with its destiny nor at peace with
itself. Its greatest exponent has been Beethoven,
and, if I am to illustrate its character by an example,
the example I should select would, perhaps, be the
third movement of his ninth symphony.

Now it must at once be conceded that Handel's
genius is but faintly tinged with this special emotional
colour. He was an unrivalled master of direct and
simple sentiment; of love, fear, triumph, mourning;
of patriotism untroubled by scruples, and of religion
that knows no doubts. But he was in no sense
modern. He no more anticipated a succeeding age in
the character of the emotions to which he sought to
give expression than in the technical methods which
he employed to express them. To many this may
seem matter of regret. With some it is undoubtedly
the cause why Handel's work arouses in them but a
cold and imperfect sympathy. Yet for my own part
I cannot wish it otherwise. To each stage in the

long development of art there is an appropriate glory.
I do not grudge it to those who are the first heralds
of a new order of things, in whose work is visible the
earliest flush of a fresh artistic dawn. But it is not
for them that I feel disposed to reserve my enthusiasm.
It is for those who have brought to the highest perfection a style which, because perfected, must have
been probably in the main inherited,—who have
pressed out of it every possibility of excellence that
it contained,—and who leave to their successors, if
these must need attempt the same task, no alternative
but to perform it worse. Of such was Handel. And
rather than lament that, living in the first half of the
eighteenth century, he did not anticipate the peculiar
triumphs of the nineteenth, let us with more reason
wonder at what he succeeded in accomplishing.
Among the many excellent qualities of the early
Georgian epoch spiritual fervour has never yet been
reckoned. Yet in the age of Voltaire and of Hume,
Handel produced the most profoundly religious music
which the world has yet known. Among the many
delightful qualities of its literature, sublimity has
not hitherto been counted. Yet in the age of Pope
and of Swift Handel conceived works whose austere

grandeur has never been surpassed.   This is an
astonishing fact.   We should have expected, judging
from analogy, that the music of that period would
have shown excellent, if somewhat artificial, work-
manship;   that it would never have aspired to
dangerous heights, or been apt to fall below a certain
and by no means contemptible level; that it would
have kept within rather narrow limits, but that
inside those limits it would have been admirable.
And, indeed, these things are true of much of
Handel's work and of that of his contemporaries.
But what we should never have anticipated is that
at the very moment that Pope was producing the
most finished of his satires, music should have been
performed in London which, in the qualities of
imagination and sublimity, we cannot parallel in the
literary world without going back to "Paradise Lost."

An attempt has been made to claim Handel as an
Englishman, and no doubt he was so more truly
than Gluck and Cherubini were Frenchmen.   But
though by choice, by tastes, by formal adoption, and
by prolonged residence he was a British subject, yet,
as Hanover was the country of his birth, and as
Germany and Italy were his teachers, it would seem

as if the part which England played in the story of his career was reduced to the comparatively humble one of paying his pensions during life and raising monuments to him after death. Something more than this, however, remains to be said. The development of genius, as of everything else, depends as much upon what it is now the fashion to call "environment" as upon its innate capabilities. Had Handel's lot been cast, as it might so easily have been, at some German Court; had he been organist at Hamburg, or capellmeister at Dresden, the greatest work of his life would in all probability never have been accomplished. Operas, concertos, harpsichord suites, church cantatas, and Passion music we should doubtless have had, as indeed we have them now. But "Israel," the "Messiah," "Samson," the immortal series of oratorios, secular and sacred, which gave him his peculiar and undivided glory would, so far as we can judge, never have been produced. To be sure, it might be maintained that England's claim to having encouraged the production of oratorio is the somewhat negative one of having declined to listen any more to opera. But this is only a part o the truth, and the least favourable part. While in

France oratorio has always proved a feeble and unhealthy exotic, England has been its natural home. Throughout the century and a half that have elapsed since "Esther" was first publicly performed in London, it has been largely with a view to the English market that the great German masters have written their choral compositions in this style. The libretto of the "Creation" was a translation from the English; the published score was half subscribed for in England, and it was performed in England within two years of its completion. Beethoven's "Mount of Olives," though the libretto has never suited English taste, was performed here as soon as the Eroica symphony by the same composer, which was first produced in Germany the same year. Spohr's "Last Judgment" was produced at the Norwich Festival. Mendelssohn's "Elijah" was written for, and first performed at, Birmingham; and it may be said generally that while other German masterpieces have too often conquered the public taste in this country by slow degrees and after long delays, oratorio has frequently taken it by storm. This, then, is England's claim to a share in the glories of Handel's achievements. And the claim is no slight one. If he learned elsewhere all that the great organ school of Germany and the theatrical and instrumental schools of Italy could teach him, it was here, and here only, that he obtained or could have obtained a full opportunity of putting the combined lessons in practice; here, and here only, was there a public ready to accept for its entertainment something that was neither Church cantata nor secular opera, but which united into a far more admirable whole the diverse excellences of both.

In the criticism which I have here attempted of Handel's work I have refrained intentionally from alluding, except in the most casual manner, to his great contemporary, Sebastian Bach. This somewhat difficult act of self-denial was not performed without a motive. Nature herself seems to suggest a parallel; for never before nor since has she given to one generation two musicians whose work is hewn on so grand a scale. Yet this particular process of comparison, inevitable as soon as Bach began to be really understood, has been almost wholly unprofitable. When it has been said that they were born in the same country, and in the same year; that they shared the sterling virtues of the German midde class of that day; that they absorbed, and used with incompar-

able effect, all the musical learning of their age ;
that they both had quick tempers ; and that both
lost their sight, their points of likeness are wellnigh exhausted. The contrasts between them, on the
other hand, are almost too deep to be instructive.
The things to be compared are too disparate to be
comparable. Both, indeed, spoke the same musical
language. With both counterpoint and fugue were
the easiest and most familiar means of conveying
their meaning. It could not be otherwise. A modern
musician learns with weariness the contrapuntal rules,
and laboriously contrives a fugue which shall satisfy
their requirements. But he writes in a dead language.
His composition is not so much an inspiration as an
exercise. Not improbably it is a very meritorious
exercise. But it carries on the face of it the stamp
of imitation, and it bears the same relation to a fugue
of Bach's that a copy of Latin hexameters bears to a
book of the *Æneid*. What, however, is almost impossible now was almost inevitable before the middle of
the last century. In those days musicians thought
in counterpoint ; nor did they ever seem more spontaneous, or more securely in possession of the appropriate vehicle for communicating their thoughts, than

N

when they employed a form which in the hands of their modern successors is apt to seem pedantic, rigid, and intractable.

But though, from the mere fact of their being contemporaries, Handel and Bach thus inevitably employed the same idiom, the uses to which they put it were wide as the poles asunder. Their genius was utterly different. Their modes of thought were even opposed. And this it is which makes a comparison of their respective merits useless, if indeed it does not, by turning critics into partisans, make it positively pernicious. The truth is, that we are here brought face to face not with a question of *taste*, but a question of *tastes*. It would be as reasonable to try and determine which was the more admirable poet, Shakespeare or Homer, Milton or Dante. Where both have reached supreme excellence in styles which are utterly different, but which all must admit to be great, who is to pronounce judgment? Each man will, doubtless, have his cherished predilection, but who will attempt to impose it on mankind? Those who are the most devoted to one will, perhaps, be the readiest to acknowledge that they could ill afford to spare the other.

It is singular to note how fate, which endowed both these great men so richly and yet so differently, after starting them apparently on the same track, contrived to make (except in the few particulars I have mentioned) their outward circumstances as diverse as their artistic leanings. Bach never travelled beyond his native country. Handel made a protracted musical progress through Italy, and finally settled in England. Bach married twice, and had twenty children. Handel died unmarried. Bach remained the most German of Germans. Handel became a naturalised Englishman. Bach's most important position was that of " cantor " in a not very considerable German town; Handel, mixing with courtiers and nobles, reigned without a musical rival in Great Britain and Ireland, his fame spreading far beyond their limits, and (as a *composer*) surpassing that of Bach himself even in Bach's own city. This difference in their destinies prevailed even beyond the grave. Bach passed away almost unnoticed, and his memory seemed to perish with him. His wife died in want. His daughter lived to be the object of public charity. His works were scattered, and some of them have hopelessly disappeared. His grave was desecrated,

and he lies in a nameless and forgotten tomb. Far other
—to the honour of his adopted country be it said—was
the fate of Handel. He died full of fame and honour,
mourned by the nation whose hospitality he had for
so many years enjoyed. His body was laid to rest
in the Abbey, among the poets whose works he had
so often illustrated, and whose genius he had more
than equalled ; and there, from that day to this, have
been heard, at no distant intervals, strains which he
bequeathed to us for our delight. His works, religi-
ously preserved, were given before the century closed
to the world in the most magnificent edition which,
I suppose, till then had been issued in any country
of the compositions of any master. And almost at
the very time when Mozart was painfully piecing
together, at Leipsic, the half-forgotten and wholly
neglected score of the poor remains of Bach's motetts,
the first centenary of Handel's birth was being celebrated at Westminster with a splendour till then
unrivalled in musical history.

Time has done much to redress the balance. Side
by side the two great names will live as marking, in
different ways, but with equal lustre, the culminating
point of one phase of musical development. The

history of art, and assuredly the history of musical
art, does not repeat itself. As one kind of tree
succeeds another with inevitable sequence in the
virgin forests of America, so has each generation its
peculiar artistic growth, which after-ages may admire,
but which they cannot reproduce without a conscious
and but half-effectual effort of imitation. The years
that have elapsed since "Israel," the "Messiah," and
the "Mass in B" were first given to the world, have
been fruitful in musical revolutions, which make it
impossible that we should ever see anything like them
again. Handel and Bach themselves, if they returned
to earth, neither could nor would produce works in
any way resembling, possibly not equalling, their
former masterpieces. Yet, though (as musical
chronology goes) these masterpieces are old, they are
not yet antiquated. In some respects we are probably
more capable of appreciating them than the audiences
for whom they were in the first instance written ;
and Time, which has raised them up no rivals in their
own kind, has not as yet materially dulled their
charm. Will this be always so ? Will the year 1985
see a Handel tricentenary as successful and as truly
popular as the bicentenary of 1885, or the (so-called)

centenary of 1784 ?   Or will his music by that time
have sunk into the purely honorary dignity of an
historic curiosity, to be discussed learnedly, to be
treated reverently, to be heard in public not at all ?

It is hard to say. Literary immortality is an
unsubstantial fiction devised by literary artists for
their own especial consolation. It means, at the
best, an existence prolonged through an infinitesimal
fraction of that infinitesimal fraction of the world's
history during which man has played his part upon
it. And, during this fraction of a fraction, what,
or rather how many things, does it mean ? A work
of genius begins by appealing to the hearts of men ;
moving their fancy, warming their imagination, entering into their inmost life.   In this period immortality
is still young ; and life really means living.   But this
condition of things has never yet endured.   What at
first was the delight of nations declines by slow but
inevitable gradation into the luxury, or the business,
or even the vanity of a few.   What once spoke in
accents understood by all is now painfully spelt out
by a small band of scholars.   What was once read
for pleasure is now read for curiosity.   It becomes
"an interesting illustration of the taste of a bygone

age," a "remarkable proof of such and such a theory of æsthetics." "It still repays perusal by those who have sufficient historic sympathy to look at it from the proper point of view," and so on. The love of those who love it best is largely alloyed with an interest which is half antiquarian and half scientific. It is no longer Tithonus in his radiant youth, gazed at with the passion-lit eyes of Luna, but Tithonus in extremest age reported on as a most remarkable and curious case by a Committee of the Royal College of Physicians.

It may be thought, perhaps, that on one or two names in literature is conferred, not merely the privilege of never dying, but the privilege of never growing old. I will not discuss a point so remote from my present theme. We cannot, unfortunately, obtain a return of the number of persons who are as familiar with Homer's Greek as a dweller on the sea-board of the Ægean in the tenth century B.C., nor of the proportion of those possessing that accomplishment who use it with a like confiding simplicity, unmoved in their credulous enjoyment of the poetic narrative by the clamour of contending critics, or the accumulated scepticism of thirty centuries. Let it be granted, then, for the sake of argument, that Homer is gifted with eternal youth, but let none expect a like destiny for even the greatest among musicians. Physical decay slowly despoils us of the masterpieces of painting. Artistic evolution will even more surely despoil us of the masterpieces of music. Let us, then, rejoice that we live in an age to whose ears the sublimest creations of the modern imagination, in the only art which owes nothing to antiquity, have not yet grown flat and unprofitable; that we are not driven to rake painfully among the ashes of the past in order to detect some faint traces of that fire of inspiration which once dazzled the world; that for us "Israel" and the "Messiah" are still "immortal," because they live in our affections, not because they lie in honourable sepulture upon the shelves of our museums.

IV

COBDEN AND THE MANCHESTER SCHOOL[1]

MR. MORLEY'S long-expected volumes are the last and most important addition to the literature, already of considerable extent, which is devoted, more or less directly, to elucidating the life and work of Cobden. The writings and speeches of this distinguished public man, supplemented by the biographical notices of friends and disciples, have for some time placed at the disposal of the public very sufficient material for estimating his character; and probably the estimate, whatever it may have been, will not be changed in any important particular by the information contained in the new biography. Nevertheless this work is far from being a superfluous addition to recent history.

[1] *Nineteenth Century,* Jan. 1882.

It does not supply us indeed with the same kind of literary enjoyment which Mr. Trevelyan has provided for us in his *Life of Macaulay*. Nor ought we to expect it. Cobden does not furnish any material for a biographer like that of which Mr. Trevelyan had made such admirable use,— for though effective both as a writer and speaker, he is never by any chance brilliant. Nor, again, need any one seek in Cobden's correspondence for new lights upon the character and motives of his contemporaries. Except during the negotiations which preceded the French Treaty, he had few opportunities of confidential intercourse with other statesmen and party leaders : and he was not perhaps of a temperament to make much use even of the opportunities which he had ; so that his observations on individuals or parties do not, as a rule, illustrate any person's character but his own. Nevertheless, in spite of these inevitable deficiencies, a book which gives us Cobden's political opinions, not as they appear full dressed in his speeches and pamphlets, but as they are to be found freely expressed in his familiar correspondence, must be both important and interesting. And this Mr. Morley has certainly provided for us. The selections from a voluminous correspondence seem to be excellently made. And Mr. Morley has taken care that his own opinions, while sufficiently enunciated, shall not occupy an unduly large share of space: a reticence for which his readers may be the more grateful, since, during the composition of his work, he would seem, from his occasional utterances, to have been in a frame of mind much more suited to the pamphleteer than to the historian.

Cobden's career, if interesting for no other reason, would be so for this, that it differs in outline—is framed, so to speak, on a different plan —from that of every other man who has risen to eminence in English political life. It was unusual in its commencement, in its course, and in its culmination. Most men desirous of a share in the direction of public affairs regard a Parliamentary seat as the first, and a certain measure of Parliamentary success as the second, requisite for giving practical effect to their political creed; while they look to office as the most effective instrument for turning the power which they may so obtain to the best account.

If this be the normal course of an English statesman, Cobden's course was abnormal in every particular. His political importance depended upon causes among which position in the House of Commons was the smallest. The most triumphant moment of his public life—the day on which the Bill repealing the Corn Laws received the Royal assent—occurred before he had sat through a whole Parliament; and it is doubtful whether it would have occurred a day later, or if he would have had a title to a smaller share in the result, had he never been a member of Parliament at all. Similar observations, though with considerable qualification, might be made respecting his career generally. Throughout his life he was always more concerned in advancing some special object or in enforcing some single idea than in taking a varied part in the complex business of government; and therefore it was that he did not regard either Parliament or office as essential instruments for carrying out his purposes. Office might too easily become a restraint; Parliament could not be more than a superior "stump" from which the favourite opinion might be advocated.

Cobden therefore must be looked on rather as a political missionary than as a statesman, as an agitator rather than as an administrator. But he was, for the particular objects he had in view, and for the particular audiences he had to address, the most effective of missionaries and the greatest of agitators. Mr. Morley puts him in this respect second to O'Connell, but in truth it is impossible to draw a comparison between them. O'Connell would have been as powerless among the middle class of Lancashire and the West Riding as Cobden would have been among the excitable peasantry of Ireland. All large audiences are moved more through their feelings than their reason. But an English multitude differs from an Irish one in preferring that appeals to its feelings should at least have the external appearance of argument; and in the art of making such appeals Cobden was a master who has never been surpassed.

The most superficially striking fact about this career of political propagandism is the very different measure of success which it met with in its first and in its second part. It is not too much perhaps to say that the Cobden of 1850–60 owed the greater part of his authority in the national councils to the reputation acquired by the Cobden of 1841–46. Men listened with respect to the untiring advocate of peace and disarmament because he was the same man who had so effectually preached against "monopolies." But they listened without conviction, and he preached without success. In 1845 Sir Louis Malet is able to describe him, not very accurately indeed, but without any glaring absurdity, as the "tribune of the people." Ten years had not elapsed before he sank from being the tribune of the people to being the unpopular adherent of a small and powerless sect, wholly unable to influence the course of events, and scarcely able to obtain a hearing except in the House of Commons, an assembly which Cobden ungratefully declared to be "packed" in the interests of that class whom he regarded it as his special mission to oppose.

This striking change, which reached its dramatic climax in 1857, when the so-called Manchester School was for an instant deprived of political existence, deserves explanation. It cannot be said that the general arguments in favour of peace and disarmament were either more difficult to understand or appealed to feebler motives than the arguments in favour of cheap bread. Both the one and the other were primarily (I do not say exclusively) directed to plain and obvious feelings of self-interest—a mode of persuasion of which Cobden always had the highest opinion.[1] Neither is it the fact that the advocates showed less zeal and less courage on the second occasion than on the first; for the zeal of the "Peace Party" was great, and their courage beyond all praise. Nor yet can it be alleged that their criticism on the prevailing policy was right between 1840 and 1850, and wholly wrong between 1850 and 1860, since few will, I suppose, be found prepared to defend in its entirety the foreign policy of the Liberal and Coalition Ministries during those years.

Mr. Bright, in 1857, when his party collapsed, offered an explanation—indeed, two explanations—of the problem. The first[2] he saw in the "ignorance, scurrility, selfishness, ingratitude, and all the unpleasant qualities that every honest politician must meet with" when he "does his duty;" while the second is given in the following sentence,

[1] Vol. ii. p. 115.   [2] *Ibid.* p. 194.

which I extract from a letter to Cobden of that date:[1] "In the sudden break-up of 'the school' of which we have been the chief professors, we may learn how far we have been, and are, ahead of the public opinion of our time. We purpose not to make a trade of politics;" and so on.

Some less simple explanation, however, seems to be required than that "the school" was honest and enlightened, while other people were "ignorant, scurrilous, selfish, and ungrateful." Politicians, following this example, need never find any difficulty in placing their conduct in an interesting light, whatever view the public may happen to take of it. Are they the popular favourites? Then are they the representatives, the tribunes, of the people, and speak almost with the voice of inspiration. Does the people burn them in effigy? It is a sign and measure of the extent to which they are ahead of the public opinion of their time.

> The people's voice is odd,
> It is, and it is not, the voice of God.

With all deference, then, to the high authorities on the other side, it appears to me that the principal

[1] Vol. ii. p. 194.

causes of the profound divergence between the
general feeling and the opinions of Cobden and his
colleagues during the last fourteen years of his life,
are to be found in the peculiar conditions of the
period in which they began their public life—conditions which, themselves transient and exceptional,
have yet profoundly and perhaps permanently
affected the course of English politics.

In ordinary times and under ordinary circumstances there is no reason why the line of political
"cleavage" should in any way coincide with the
difference between the manufacturing and the agricultural interest. The fact that one man has his
property invested in land and farm-buildings, and
another in plant and machinery, does not in the
nature of things supply a sufficient reason for their
belonging to different political parties. The period,
however, when Cobden first took interest in public
affairs, was in this respect not ordinary. The very
imperfect representation of the great manufacturing
centres, which it was the chief and perhaps the only
merit of the first Reform Bill to have remedied, left
a certain soreness even after it had disappeared.
When to the memory of this former grievance was

o

added the consciousness of an existing wrong—when it was shown that in the interests of the class who had too long retained an undue share of political power, laws were in force which favoured their material prosperity at the expense of those very persons who had just been admitted to a full share of Parliamentary influence—it is evident that the conditions existed under which ordinary party warfare might be complicated by a struggle between the manufacturers and agriculturalists, or, as Cobden chose to put it, between the middle classes and the aristocracy. These were facts which the philosophic Radicals (who to a certain extent prepared the way for their more robust brethren of the Manchester School) were perfectly ready to demonstrate. Their politics made them dislike the landlords, their political economy made them dislike the Corn Laws, and they were ready to supply any amount of abstract reasoning in favour of a policy which might impoverish the one by destroying the other. Abstract reasoning, however, though not to be despised as an ally, is by itself the feeblest of political forces. If Protection had embraced the whole circle of our industries, or if it had been used to keep up the price of anything but the necessaries of life, fragments of it might have survived to this day, in spite of all the demonstrations in the world. But it so happened that the great change in our fiscal system in the direction of Free Trade had already begun in the pre-Reform period under Lord Liverpool, and had *not* begun with agriculture. It was inevitable, therefore, that the manufacturers should ask why Parliament in dealing with the articles they produced should legislate in favour of the consumer, while in dealing with the articles they consumed it should legislate in favour of the producer; and this question, though not more difficult to answer, became much more difficult to ignore when commerce was declining, poor-rates rising, and wheat cost seventy-seven shillings a quarter.

The interest of all this, so far as Cobden is concerned, lies in the fact that instead of entering into political life merely as a member of one of the two great political parties, he entered it to fight a manufacturer's, or as he called it, a middle - class battle, against "aristocratic monopolists," with arguments drawn from an abstract science.   These circumstances modified profoundly, and, as I think, perniciously, the whole course of his public life. They fostered the habit of regarding all political controversies as controversies between classes; so that (among other evil effects) to all the bitternesses which arise from political disagreement was added all the bitternesses which arise from real or imaginary social divisions. They induced him to rate too highly the importance of purely economic considerations in deciding questions of general policy, and to misinterpret or ignore some of the most powerful and by no means the most contemptible, motives by which the history of nations is influenced. They were, perhaps, the real causes of the un-English character attributed to his school of statesmanship by Mr. Disraeli, and which Mr. Bright, while he confessed to it, characteristically claimed as an indication of its superior honesty and public spirit.

Those who are desirous to observe how these causes conspired together to warp Cobden's political speculations, may note his theory of "the aristocracy," a theory almost as important in his political system as is the law of gravitation in astronomy. Mr. Morley appears entirely to share his hero's views on this subject, and his two volumes through-

out presuppose a version of the drama of English
history, according to which a selfish, unscrupulous,
and feudal aristocracy figures sometimes as the villain,
and sometimes as the fool of the piece, alternately
coercing, robbing, and corrupting a weak but
estimable middle class. "Selfish," "insolent,"
"corrupt," "depraved," "prejudiced," "stupid," "viru-
lent," "unscrupulous," "hypocritical," "unprincipled,"
are some of the expressions Mr. Morley is impelled
to employ, in order to do justice to his own and
his friend's views of landlords and aristocrats, protectionist or otherwise; and though Cobden is more
moderate in his language, he is scarcely more reasonable in his opinions. We are not, it must be remembered, dealing now with the rhetorical devices—
the "violations of good taste and kind feeling"—
which Cobden said [1] he found necessary in order
that audiences which declined to come merely to be
instructed might be "excited, flattered, and pleased";
nor yet with the outbursts of that irritable in-
tolerance, which, as displayed by one member of
the school, so strangely remind Mr. Morley [2]
of the "wrath of an ancient prophet." We are

[1] Vol. i. p. 194.   [2] *Ibid.* p. 207.

concerned with a theory which was gravely held by
the leaders of the "Manchester School," which
modified all their political judgments and supplied
them with a key to all the mysteries of comtempor-
ary politics.   According to this the population of
England might be divided, not only socially but for
all political purposes, into three classes — upper,
middle, and lower.   The interests of the middle and
lower classes were identical, and were both opposed
to the interests of the upper class.   Nevertheless it
was the upper class which governed the country.   It
refused to admit any members of the other classes
to a share in the direction of affairs.   It liked large
armaments, because they supported the younger
children of landlords.   It liked war, because war
justifies large armaments.   It liked an active foreign
policy, because that always conduces to war.   Its
very existence was a standing violation of the
"principles of political economy."

This singular theory was probably derived in
part from the doctrinaire school of political economists, who having divided the produce of agriculture
into rent, profit, and wages, and having asserted,
truly enough, that rent *as defined by them* was not

earned either by labour or abstinence, were apt to
regard its existence as an economic accident, unfortunately taken advantage of by a small and not
very useful portion of the community.   It is evident,
also, that Cobden's views on this subject were
largely influenced by his own strong class feeling.
He chose to regard the manufacturers as a distinct
"order" in the State, and he chose to regard "the
aristocracy" as another and rival "order."   One of
his early aspirations[1] was to see the commercial
classes "become the De Medicis, Fuggers, and De
Witts of England, instead of glorying in being the
toadies of a clodpole aristocracy only less enlightened
than themselves."   And many years later he expressed, in not less polished language, vehement
indignation against the manufacturers of Manchester,
who declined to be represented by so valiant a
defender of their "order" as Mr. John Bright.[2]

The principal cause, however, of Cobden's "class
theory" of English politics is, I believe, to be
found in the Corn Law controversy;—and at first
sight the circumstances of this struggle might
seem to supply not only a sufficient motive, but

[1] Vol. i. p. 194.   [2] *Ibid.* p. 197.

an adequate justification of it. For while there could be no doubt that the leaders of the Protectionists were landlords, it was also true that their interests were involved in maintaining the protective system, while the interests of the urban portion of the community lay on the whole in its abolition. Here, if anywhere, might seem to exist a state of things which would justify the epithets of which I gave above an imperfect, though sufficient catalogue.

In truth, however, a sober examination of the facts of English politics, between the formation of the League and the abolition of the Corn Laws, is quite sufficient to show that the government of England was not then, any more than at previous periods of our history, aristocratic in any proper sense of that term, and that the class whom Cobden chose to describe as the aristocracy, were not open to the charges of unscrupulous selfishness which it pleased him and his school frequently to bring against them.

It is absurd to ascribe corrupt motives to large bodies of men, merely because the economic theories they adopt are in accordance with their own interests.   No one doubts the purity of Cobden's motives in promoting the Corn Law agitation. Yet Cobden not only believed that the profits of his ordinary business would be greatly augmented by the changes he advocated, but went out of his way to speculate in town land, on the ground that its value must rise as soon as the tax on bread was abolished.   It may be said that the motives of the Protectionists were liable to suspicion because their theories were not only favourable to themselves, but were manifestly false.   But at this moment the vast majority of the civilised world advocate false economic theories of precisely the same kind; and of that majority, the great majority imagine those theories to be to their own advantage.   The civilised world may possibly be foolish : but not, surely, unscrupulous and hypocritical.   Why are the English landlords of 1845 to be described in harsher language than the English manufacturers of 1821, or the French, American, German, Russian, Canadian, and Australian manufacturers of 1881 ?   Their error may be a proof of stupidity, but if it be, the stupidity is too general to excite either surprise or indignation.

In truth, however, it was hardly open to Cobden to charge the Protectionists with stupidity. Though not, so far as appears, a very profound political economist himself, he was of opinion that political economy was more difficult of comprehension than any of the "exact sciences." Which of the exact sciences he had mastered (unless phrenology be one) Mr. Morley does not, so far as I recollect, inform us. But at all events the majority of mankind cannot be expected to understand the exact sciences, and are not to be described as selfishly foolish when they fail to do so.

But Cobden committed a much more serious error than that of merely misjudging the motives of his political opponents :—he misjudged their political position. When he represented the Corn Laws as examples of the pernicious class legislation, which, together with wars and armaments, we owed to the fact that we have long been governed by a "feudal aristocracy," he used language admirably suited indeed to further his agitation, but not at all fitted to encourage, either in himself or his hearers, a true perception of the facts.

In the first place it is as certain as anything in hypothetical history can be, that Corn Laws would have existed in England, however property in land had happened to be distributed. If the soil had been owned in small lots, protection would have been demanded, and given, as surely as it was under the actual circumstances; but it would not have been so easily removed. Cobden, as we have seen, shared to the full the dislike of his school to large landed properties. In this he was ungrateful. It was the existence of large landed properties that ensured and accelerated the great triumph of his life. Does any one imagine that any important minority of a peasant proprietary would have been converted to the doctrine of Free Trade? Or that any minority at all would have supported a bill calculated to reduce them by thousands to beggary and ruin? Owing to the existence of a "feudal aristocracy" those most permanently, if not most deeply, interested in the continuance of a tax on bread were few; they were not united; and the question to them was not one of life and death. Had the soil been parcelled out among small owners, all these conditions would have been reversed.

The country would have been arrayed against the towns, powerful, perhaps overwhelming in numbers, entirely of one mind, undisturbed by any knowledge of the "exact sciences," and determined by hard necessity to fight to the last. How, and at what cost, would such a struggle have ended?

In the second place, it cannot be doubted that the Protectionist landlords, so far from fighting, as Cobden would say, solely for their "order," represented the middle classes of the counties as faithfully as did Cobden and the leaders of the League the middle classes of the towns. That the landlords have ever in English history constituted, in any accurate sense of the term, a political aristocracy, is indeed a pure illusion. An aristocracy is a class which governs independently of, and if need be in opposition to, public opinion. There has never been any such government in this country. It is not of course denied that in England the owners of the soil have been a powerful body; nor should I dispute the fact that the same public opinion from which, in the main, they derived their power may possibly have in some cases permitted it to be used, consciously or unconsciously, for purposes more to their

advantage than to that of the community at large.
It can hardly be otherwise. The government which
does not occasionally sacrifice a general advantage
feebly coveted to the wishes of a class powerfully
expressed, has yet to be discovered. But this
disease is incident to all forms of government by
public opinion. Whatever the nominal form of such
government may be, whether it be called republican
or monarchical, whether it has a less or a more restricted suffrage, there will always be classes in it
whose members have greater power than any equal
number of its other citizens taken at random. These
classes may consist of landowners or millowners,
journalists or wirepullers. Their power may be
exercised on the whole for good, or on the whole for
evil. It may arise from temporary or from enduring
causes. It may be obtained by historical accident, by
intrigue, by merit, by utility to a faction or by obse-
quiousness to a mob. But however it be acquired, or
however it be used, it is certain to exist. It must be
observed, indeed, that this class power is of very
different kinds. It may belong to a class in its cor-
porate capacity, acting as a united body. Such is
the power of the railway "interest" or of the "Irish

vote." It may belong to a class because the individuals composing that class, or many of them, are possessed of special sources of influence, as, for example, editors of newspapers or large employers of labour; or it may belong to a class, because its members, possessing leisure, local position, or some other quality which commends them as fitting candidates to the constituencies, are largely chosen as the exponents of public opinion, or of some important section of public opinion. Cobden too often forgot the extent to which the class whom he chose to describe as "the aristocracy" obtained their power in this third or derivative manner. He was by this initial mistake constantly led into errors of judgment regarding the nature of the political forces with which he had to deal. During the continuance of the Corn Law controversy, this was of small moment. It added greatly to the force and point of his rhetoric to represent the hated "monopoly" as imposed by the power, and retained in the interests, of a small, a selfish, and a wealthy minority; and the opinion, though absurd, led to no practical inconveniences. But when this question was disposed of, his theory led him sometimes into strange mistakes.

In 1848 he feared a war with France[1] owing to the
"natural repugnance on the part of our Government,
composed as it is entirely of the aristocracy, to go on
cordially with a republic." In the next year we
find him writing to Mr. Bright,[2] "I wish to abate
the power of the aristocracy in their strongholds.
Our enemy is subtle and powerful," etc. By 1852,
however, *à propos* of the Militia Bill, he began somewhat more clearly to recognise that wickedness and
folly were not confined entirely to high places. "All
the aristocratic parties," he says,[3] "are in favour of
more armaments. Our business is to try and make
the people of a different opinion. I am more and
more convinced that we have much to do with the
public, before we can, with any sense or usefulness,
quarrel with this or that aristocratic party." The
next year, this not very recondite fact seems to be
clearly apprehended. "Before you and I," he writes,[4]
"find fault with the Whig chiefs, let us ask ourselves
candidly whether the country at large is in favour of
any other policy than that which has been pursued
by the aristocracy, Whig and Tory, for the last

[1] Vol. ii. p. 17.   [2] *Ibid.* p. 57.
[3] *Ibid.* p. 114.   [4] *Ibid.* p. 132.

century and a half." Yet when the crash came in
1857, the hardly learnt truth is forgotten. Cobden
was unable to believe that the middle classes and "the
aristocracy" could honestly agree to differ with him.
Some other explanation had to be sought for the
total collapse of the Manchester School, and that
explanation he found in the degradation of the class
in whom he had been accustomed to put his trust.
Prompted by the same spirit of enlightened charity
which suggested the statement [1] that the wickedness
and folly of unnecessary wars could not be avoided,
because without the expenditure on "wars and
armaments" the "aristocracy could not endure," [2]

[1] Vol. ii. p. 362 (respecting the China War of 1860).

[2] In reference to this favourite accusation of the Manchester
School, it may interest the reader to note (1) that Mr. Morley
tells us (vol. ii. p. 444) that in 1864 "the supreme control of
peace and war was finally taken out of the hands of the old terri-
torial oligarchy;" (2) that he is of opinion (vol. ii. p. 378)
that the "Liberal awakening" which "placed Mr. Gladstone in
power, with Mr. Bright himself for the most popular and
influential of his colleagues," put the country in a condition to deal
properly with the expenditure on armaments, which could not be
done in 1862 owing to "the ignorance and flunkeyism of the
middle classes;" (3) that the army and navy estimates are now
(1882) bigger than ever. I may confess that I used to believe
that the stupid calumny to which I allude in the text was an
invention unscrupulously used for party purposes. I must
sincerely apologise for this silent injustice, which had its origin
in the fact that the theory in question seemed to be too foolish to

he suggests a not less wicked but even more contemptible reason for the adherence of the "middle classes" to the policy of the "upper." As the latter are, according to Cobden's theory, influenced by greed of money, so the former are influenced by subservience to rank. The manufacturers of Manchester who presumed to turn out Mr. Bright are[1] "base snobs," who "kick away the ladder" by which they have risen to prosperity, and their action is characterised[2] as "a display of snobbishness and ingratitude." A friend makes a failure in seconding the Address. Upon which Cobden writes:[3] "I have never known a manufacturing representative put into a cocked hat and breeches and ruffles, with a sword by his side, to make a speech for Government, without having his head turned by the feathers and frippery. Generally they give way to a paroxysm of snobbery, and go down on their bellies, and throw dust on their heads, and fling dirt at the prominent men of their own order."

It is some comfort to think that in this dark

be credited by men of sense and education. I gladly yield to the conclusive evidence to the contrary which is furnished by the private correspondence of Mr. Cobden.

[1] P. 197.   [2] P. 198.   [3] P. 198.

picture of the meanness of "the only class (as Cobden said[1]) from whose action in his time any beneficial changes were to be expected," some brighter spots are to be found. Prone as the middle classes are to be[2] "timid and servile" to the "feudal governing class," yet in one favoured spot more masculine qualities are still to be found among them. In August 1857, shortly after his rejection for Manchester, Mr. Bright was elected for Birmingham. The people of Birmingham, it is reassuring to learn,[3] are "honest and independent," and "free from aristo-cratic snobbery."

We could have, I think, no more striking example than this of the extent to which Cobden's judgment of men was perverted by his inveterate habit of looking at every question from the point of view of class divisions. Making all allowance for the irritation caused by a crushing defeat not very philosophically endured, is there not something very foolish, and I had almost said a little vulgar, in thus attributing the catastrophe to the overmastering influence of the meanest and vulgarest of motives? Grant that Lord Palmerston was entirely in the

---

[1] P. 390.   [2] P. 396.   P. 199.

wrong about the China War; grant that the combination of parties which forced him to dissolve was entirely in the right; is the theory credible, is it even plausible, which represents the political forces which sent him back to office after the general election, as being the infamous cupidity of one section of the community and the contemptible meanness of another? Is it impossible that for some, even for most political purposes, social divisions should be neglected? Is it impossible that the general opinion of all classes should be swayed by one set of motives? Is it impossible that those motives should be respectable?

In all this the influence of the fact that Cobden's early political battles really were class contests is sufficiently apparent. The other circumstance I pointed out, namely, that those battles were fought for commercial objects and on economic grounds, had even more effect on the character and influence of the opinions which he spent the latter portion of his life in advocating.

Some lady, in 1852, remarked that Cobden's policy never rose beyond a "bagman's millennium." This observation, uttered in private, and in the freedom of conversation, was not untrue for an epigram, and

was both more just and more charitable than some
of the judgments (by no means epigrammatic) which
in these volumes Mr. Morley has written down,
printed, corrected for the press, and published. His
comments on the observation are in these terms:[1]—

This was the clever way among the selfish and insolent
of saying, that the ideal which Cobden cherished was
comfort for the mass, not luxury for the few. He knew
much better than they (*i.e.* the class " whose lives are one
long course of indolence, dilettantism, and sensuality ")[2]
that material comfort is, as little as luxury, the highest
satisfaction of man's highest capacities, but he could well
afford to scorn the demand for fine ideals of life on the
lips of a class who were starving the workers of the
country in order to save their own rents.

Mr. Morley is angry but confused. The second
sentence of his criticism shows that he understands
the nature of the complaint urged by the " insolent
and selfish " against Cobden's views of national
policy ; so that the first sentence must be regarded
as a deliberate perversion of it. As for the last
clause, it is as impossible to see why Cobden should
scorn a demand which he knew to be just because he
objected to the lips which uttered it, as to discover

[1] Vol. i. p. 207. [2] *Ibid.* p. 206.

how, in 1852, six years after the abolition of the
Corn Laws, it was possible " to save rents by starving
the workers of the country."

What, then, was the policy of which it is so dangerous to hint disapprobation? Cobden's admirers
sometimes talk as if he was the discoverer of the fact
that war is expensive, that when it is unnecessary it
is not only expensive but wicked, and that the nation
which does that which is expensive and wicked is
certain to suffer both in purse and morals. His
opponents, on the other hand, sometimes represent
him as advocating peace under all circumstances and
under every provocation; or, as it is called, " peace at
any price." As a matter of fact he did something
more important than preach the commonplaces for
which the first applaud him, and something less
absurd than support the paradox which the second
lay to his charge. It is true that these last seem
almost justified by the impartial and universal disapproval with which Cobden regarded everything
which could by any possibility promote what he
called " the military spirit." He not only thought
that every modern war in which this country has
ever been engaged was wholly indefensible, but he

regarded with the darkest suspicion every instrument by which war, whether offensive or defensive, could by any possibility be carried on. He wished to cut down the army and the navy; he objected to the militia; he attacked the volunteers; and he vehemently disapproved of every fortification scheme that was proposed.

But behind all this criticism of war and warlike expenditure there lay a theory of the British Empire which, if accepted, would go far to account for Cobden's views respecting armaments, but which the English people did not accept in Cobden's lifetime, and do not accept now. It was this fundamental divergence which rendered it inevitable that his reiterated attacks on the military policy of successive governments should fail of their effect, and made the best-founded objections liable to a natural suspicion that they rested on presuppositions with which his hearers could not agree. Cobden's view of the external relations of our Empire was purely commercial and economic; in the language of the "selfish and insolent," the view of a bagman. "He delighted," says Mr. Morley,[1] "in such businesslike statements

[1] Vol. i. p. 98.

as that the cost of the Mediterranean Squadron, in proportion to the amount of trade which it was professedly employed to protect, was as though a merchant should find that his traveller's expenses for escort alone were to amount to 6s. 8d. in the pound on the amount of his sales." In something of the same spirit he estimated the value of our foreign possessions. In order to be worth keeping they must pay, and pay in a manner as easily demonstrable as the profits of a bank or the yield of a mine. Not only must they pay, but it must be shown that they would not pay as well if they belonged to somebody else; and on this point Cobden was not easy to convince. The author of the Commercial Treaty with France was of opinion that the manufacturers of Manchester exhibited a melancholy ignorance[1] of the principles of Free Trade when they viewed with alarm the possibility of India passing to another, and, as he must have known, a protectionist power. "Now that the trade of Hindostan," he says,[2] "is thrown open to all the world on equal terms, what exclusive advantage can we derive to compensate for all the trouble,

[1] Vol. ii. p. 214.   [2] *Ibid.* p. 206.

cost, and risk of ruling over such a people?" And again: [1] "Under the *régime* of Free Trade Canada is not a whit more ours than the United States." Inspired by these opinions, he would have seen India go with pleasure, the colonies without regret. They cost money to defend; and we got nothing for the privilege of defending them but commercial advantages which we should equally possess if they had to defend themselves.

Now I do not mean to discuss the effect which the loss of our Indian and colonial possessions would have on our trade, though I think Cobden underrated and greatly underrated it; nor yet the evil consequences of severance to the dependencies themselves, which Cobden denied or left out of account. The interesting point is to note how apt he was to ignore for himself, and to misinterpret in others, every view of the Empire which was not exclusively commercial. To him our vast and scattered dominions appeared to be an ill-constructed fabric, built at the cost of much innocent blood and much ill-spent treasure, and which, having been originally contrived in obedience to a mistaken theory of trade,

---

[1] Vol. ii. p. 42.

was not worth the trouble of keeping in repair now that that theory had been finally exploded. The same deficient sympathy and insight which prevented him seeing any cause for the Napoleonic wars but the selfish ambition of the "ruling class," or any result of them but continental complications and a crushing debt, made him regard the motives which induce ordinary Englishmen obstinately to cling to the responsibilities of Empire as consisting of an uninstructed love of gain or a vulgar greed of territory. He may have been right in thinking that the weight of imperial responsibilities will become a burden too heavy to be borne. It may be true that the sceptre of dominion is doomed at no distant date to slide from our failing grasp. We may be destined, from choice or from necessity, to shut ourselves up within the four seas; and it is not absolutely impossible, though in the highest degree improbable, that even under these conditions our Board of Trade Returns may be such as to delight the heart of a Chancellor of the Exchequer. But no man is fit to estimate the consequences of these changes who attempts to estimate them solely and exclusively by figures. The sentiments with which an Englishman regards the English Empire are neither a small nor an ignoble part of the feelings which belong to him as a member of the commonwealth. If therefore that Empire is destined to dissolve, and with it all the associations by which it is surrounded; if we in these islands are henceforth to turn our gaze solely inwards upon ourselves and our local affairs; if we are to have no relations with foreigners, or with men of our own race living on other continents, except those which may be adequately expressed by double entry and exhibited in a ledger;—we may be richer or poorer for the change, but it is folly to suppose that we shall be richer or poorer only. An element will be withdrawn from our national life which, if not wholly free from base alloy, we can yet ill afford to spare; and which none, at all events, can be competent to criticise unless, unlike Mr. Cobden, they first show themselves capable of understanding it.

If Cobden's views on questions of foreign and colonial policy were somewhat narrowed by his too strictly economic view of our external relations, it was only natural that his views on all questions connected with land should be somewhat warped by his aversion to the class who owned so much of it.

One of the most amusing instances of this is a proposal he makes[1] for settling the Irish land difficulty by applying to it the law of succession as it exists in France.   Many strange remedies have been proposed for the agrarian ills of that unhappy country: some strange ones have been adopted; but surely no one before or since has professed to see the salvation of Ireland in the slow but indefinite multiplication of squireens.   It was not, however, to large landlords in Ireland only that he objected.   He professed to think[2] that a "feudal governing class" (as by a bold misuse of terms he was accustomed to describe them) "exists only in violation of sound principles of political economy."   But he left no very clear account of what he meant by the statement.   If, as might be conjectured, he was alluding to the restrictions (for the most part imaginary) on the sale and transfer of land, which are due to settlement and entail, it is sufficient to remark that no class owes its existence or its power to the continuance of these restrictions: if he meant anything else, it is difficult to see what political economy has to do with the matter.   The inquiry, however, is not very important.   Cobden

[1] Vol. ii. p. 28.   [2] *Ibid.* p. 369.

was not the first, nor will he be the last statesman who imagines that in yielding to his political or social dislikes he does honour to political economy ; and the particular form which the process of self-deception took in his case is not now of much interest even from a purely biographical point of view.

Much, then, as there is to admire in his hero, a perusal of the new material Mr. Morley has provided us with does not, I think, dissipate the impression that the eulogies of some of his disciples are excessive and overstrained. Cobden was an honest, an able, and a useful public man, but not, I think, as his admirers claim for him, either a great politician or a great political philosopher. He was prevented from being the first by the mental peculiarity which made him a serviceable ally only when (as he says himself[1]) he was advancing some "defined and simple principle"; a limitation which, whatever its compensating advantages may be, is an effectual bar to the highest success in a career which requires in those who pursue it a power of dealing not only with principles, but likewise with an infinity of practical problems which are neither "defined" *nor* "simple." He was, on the

[1] Vol. i. p. 369.

other hand, prevented from being a great political philosopher, if by no other causes, still by the circumstances of his early life. His education, pursued with admirable energy while he was immersed in the business of clerk and commercial traveller, was not, and perhaps could not be, of the kind best suited to counteract the somewhat narrowing influences which, as I have pointed out, surrounded his early political career. His radicalism from the first was the radicalism of a class, and such in all essentials it remained to the end. His lack of the historic sense was not compensated by any great scientific or speculative power. Much as he saw to disapprove of in the existing condition of England, he never framed a large and consistent theory of the methods by which it was to be improved. Outside the narrow bounds of the economics of trade he had political projects, but no coherent political system; so that if he was too theoretical to make a good minister of state, he was too fragmentary and inconsistent to make a really important theorist. For example, there was no expectation which he more confidently cherished than the amiable one that Free Trade would lead, and lead soon, to general peace. Yet there was no practical reform which, towards the end of his life, he more desired to see carried into effect than an alteration in international law which should free private property from liability to capture at sea. This was (need I say?) resisted, in his opinion, only by a "selfish aristocracy." Yet had it been adopted, Free Trade would, for this country at least, have lost its most pacific virtues. These obviously consist in the fact that Free Trade enormously increases the indirect cost of hostilities : and it is plain that if the proposed alteration in the laws of maritime warfare is to be recommended at all, it is to be recommended on the ground that, in the case of a maritime power, it destroys the indirect cost altogether. Again, he was shocked to see the English peasant "*divorced*," as the phrase is, "from the soil," or, in plain English, tilling the land for weekly wages. But he bore with the greatest composure the not less painful fact that the pitman is divorced from the mine, and the operative from the mill. He had plenty of schemes for getting rid of large landowners, but none, so far as I know, for abolishing large manufacturers. He seems to have been sensitive—morbidly sensitive—to the more or less imaginary social distinctions which, as he thought, separated the landowner from the capitalist; yet never to have perceived the very real and substantial differences by which the capitalist is divided from the operative. We can hardly regret these theoretical imperfections in a system which probably would not have been better for being more logical. In any case, the only accusation that could be brought against him is that he did not rise superior to the ordinary radicalism of the day. Let those who are inclined to take a severer view of the narrowness, prejudice, and inconsistency which in some degree marred his career as a whole, not only call to mind the great qualities by which these shortcomings were accompanied, but also recollect how happily his defects conspired with his merits to render him a fitting instrument for carrying out the inevitable change in our fiscal policy which was the most important work of his public life, and with which his name will for ever be connected.

V

POLITICS AND POLITICAL ECONOMY [1]

POLITICAL economy is somewhat at a discount. Those who preach its doctrines scarcely speak with their old assurance, neither do they who listen, listen with the old respect. Ancient heresies, long thought to have been dead and buried, are beginning to revive. New heresies are daily springing into life. Every sign seems to portend that at a time when, of all others, problems are pressing for solution, in dealing with which we must be largely guided by economic science, the guide itself is in public estimation becoming seriously discredited. Some of you may have read the not very agreeable memoirs which that not very agreeable woman, Miss Martineau, has left of

---

[1] A Non-Party Lecture delivered before the Manchester Athenæum.—*National Review*, May 1885.

herself. If so, you will probably recollect the fame and profit which her series of political economy tales brought her some fifty years ago. You will recollect how she became a literary lion of the first magnitude, how edition after edition of the tales were sold off, how high officials furnished her with information and Cabinet Ministers besought her aid. Great is the difference between 1885 and 1833. Let no aspirant for such noisy honours seek them any more by this road. Much work may, indeed, be done in the field of political economy; work in the accumulation of facts; work in their reduction to law; work in popularising the results attained. But the most successful labourers in these departments need no longer expect to dictate terms to their publishers or be asked to dine by the President of the Board of Trade. He may consider himself fortunate if the world will consent to accept the results of his labour for nothing, and if he does not hear his science relegated to Saturn by a responsible Minister of the Crown.

What are the causes which have produced this change in the public mind, how far is it justified, and what attitude ought we ourselves to take up towards it ? Such is the problem which I should wish to consider with you to-day, and no more important problem, believe me, confronts the statesman who desires to face the larger issues of contemporary politics.

I pass lightly over the superficial causes which have aided in producing this economic eclipse. Such, for example, is the unpopularity which in society the third-rate exponent of economic orthodoxy has always aroused, and which you may see exemplified in more than one character in the fiction which was contemporary with the most flourishing days of that science. The professed political economist, who had a cut-and-dried formula for every occasion, who solved all social questions by a frigid calculation, who habitually talked as if everything good in the world was produced by the accumulation of wealth and everything bad by the multiplication of children, appeared to our fathers, as, did he still flourish with all his pristine vigour, he would doubtless appear to us, to be something of a prig and a great deal of a bore. No dexterity of treatment, no literary skill, will make political economy amusing ; nor will the average of mankind ever take delight in studies which require abstract thought or concentrated attention.   When, therefore, a set of persons appeared, neither very original nor very learned, who would not permit a new tax or an amendment of the poor laws to be discussed in the lobby of the House of Commons or round a dinner-table without reproducing, with all the arrogance of conscious orthodoxy, some abstract train of reasoning borrowed from greater men than themselves, they and their science were naturally looked upon as socially intolerable.

This by itself was a comparatively small misfortune. A far greater one—one of which we have not yet felt the full effects—is the hostility which the claims of political economy have aroused in the breasts of the working-classes on the Continent.   To many of them it appears, not as a political science, but as a political device ; not as a reasoned body of truth, but as a plausible tissue of sophistries, invented in the interests of capital to justify the robbery of labour.   It is true that no such prejudice, though it exists sporadically, is prevalent in this island ; but we may, I think, detect a faint echo of it in the suspicion with which it is regarded by some, and the indifference with which it is regarded by others among those who profess more especially to be the guardians of the interests of the working-classes. And it is this suspicion and indifference, too largely shared by leading politicians on both sides, of which I desire to investigate the causes.

Of course, it may be maintained that the principal and all-sufficient cause of which we are in search is to be found in the shortcomings of political economy itself. It may be alleged that its premises are arbitrary, its conclusions unproved, its teachings of too remote and abstract a character to be any sufficient guide in the conduct of public affairs. This contention I do not mean here to dispute. To dispute it effectively would require a survey of the whole field of political economy—a restatement and justification of all its principal doctrines. Such a task I need not say that I have no intention of undertaking. I shall here assume, for the sake of argument, that political economy is to be accepted as true in the same sense that other sciences are accepted as true—that is, not blindly and irrevocably, but subject to revision and development; and that it is to be regarded as a guide in the same way that other sciences are regarded as guides, that is, with a due recognition of the fact that the complexity of nature never quite corresponds with the artificial simplicity of our premises, and that in proportion as the correspondence is imperfect, the result of our reasoning must in practice be applied with caution. The first cause, then, which I take note of, for the undue depreciation under which political economy is at this moment suffering, is the undue appreciation in which it was held in the last generation. That generation— the one preceding 1860—was emphatically the generation of economic reform. It saw the new Poor Law established, the whole system of national taxation remodelled, and the Corn Laws abolished. Coincidently with this it saw an immense increase in the wealth and prosperity of the country, partly due to these changes, still more due to the development of railways and the opening up of new countries rich in agricultural and mineral resources. What wonder that the science, under whose auspices so much of this had been done, was estimated at its full, nay, at more than its full value; that the habitual distrust of theory was for a moment lulled to rest in the Anglo-Saxon mind, and that others besides Mr. Cobden prophesied the rapid and triumphant spread of Free

Trade doctrines throughout the civilised world. The most stolidly practical were reconciled to abstract principles which, as they supposed, gave them an elastic revenue and an unshackled trade : the least educated could understand the meaning and merits of cheap bread.

But no science can become popular with impunity. The mere fact that it is quoted on hustings, that its doctrines, more or less misunderstood, are used as political weapons ; and that its conclusions, more or less garbled, are valued not so much because they are true as because they suit the momentary necessities of party warfare, refracts in countless ways the dry light in which it should be viewed. The side against whom it makes will decry it ; their opponents will laud it to the skies ; and the praise which is shouted from one set of platforms will probably be not less unintelligent than the blame shouted back from another.

Not less unintelligent, and even more injurious to the cause of truth. For as soon as any body of doctrine becomes the watchword of a party or a sect, it is certain to be used with the most confident assurance by multitudes who have the most imperfect apprehension of the true grounds of the opinions they are expressing. In default of reasons they quote authorities. A dictum of Smith, Ricardo, or Mill is supposed to supply a rule of faith against which there is no appeal. A standard of orthodoxy is set up, to deviate from which is heresy, and political economy ceases to be a living science, and petrifies into an unchanging creed. From these causes has proceeded the reaction against economic teaching, which has been slowly gaining ground since 1860. Some have been repelled by the ignorant dogmatism and the narrow formalism which so often usurped the name of science. Others have been shaken in their faith by the rejection both of the theory and the practice of Free Trade by foreign countries; a still larger number have felt themselves injured by the operation of Free Trade in our own. While its friends have thus been cooled in their allegiance, its enemies have multiplied in number and increased in courage; and all those who saw in the accepted truths of political economy an obstacle to some project of their own, have been encouraged to attack it openly or by implication.

It is the first of these evils which it most behoves those of us who hold that the study of economic facts is a necessary preliminary to any judicious treatment of some of the most important problems of the day to remedy as far as in us lies. The true, if obvious, antidote to the disgust excited by the extravagant claims put forward on behalf of political economy, is to reduce those claims within strictly reasonable limits. Now what are those limits? Two there are, constantly violated, and sometimes by the greatest economic authorities, to which I would specially draw your attention. The first depends on the fact that political economy is a science, and as such deals in strictness only with laws of nature, and not with the rules of conduct or policy which may be founded on those laws. The second depends on a fact (too often forgotten) that the science of political economy, dealing as it does with only a few of the complex facts of life, cannot on most questions supply the politician with adequate grounds for framing his policy. Take an example. We constantly hear it said that the doctrine of *laissez-faire*—the doctrine which forbids State interference, and which asserts that all social questions should be solved by the unrestricted play of free competition, is a truth of political economy. Now I hold, first, that this is not a truth of political economy; and, secondly, that political economy by itself cannot furnish grounds for deciding whether it is a truth at all. It is not a truth of political economy, for it is not a scientific truth, but a maxim, sound or unsound, belonging to the art of politics. No doubt the grounds for accepting or rejecting it must be, and are, largely drawn from a consideration of economic laws, but in itself it is not an economic law, but a practical precept. It has no more claim to be regarded as a part of political economy than the recommendation not to throw yourself out of a second-floor window is a part of the science of mutually gravitating bodies. Do not think that the distinction here drawn is a mere subtlety. I am convinced that the neglect of it by many of the masters of the science, and by almost all their disciples, has done much to prejudice men's minds against economic reasoning. A political economist, as such, has no business to be a politician. However strong his convictions may be, however much his own inclinations may tempt him to the advocacy of any particular mode of social organisation, he should rigidly abstain, in his investigation of the laws of wealth, from loading his pages with any practical propaganda. Science is of no party. It seeks no object, selfish or unselfish, good or bad. It is unmoved by any emotion : it feels no pity, nor is it stirred by any wrong. Its sole aim is the investigation of truth and the discovery of law, wholly indifferent to the use to which those investigations and those discoveries may afterwards be put.

But this is not the only reason, nor even the chief reason, why I object to the fusion, or rather the confusion, of the art of politics with the science of political economy. Another and a more cogent one is to be found in the fact that, as I have said, many of the most important considerations which should determine a political decision lie altogether outside the field with which an economist is at liberty to deal. The economist investigates only the laws regulating the production, exchange, and distribution of wealth ; and in order to get this problem within a manageable compass, in order to avoid being confronted with calculations of hopeless complexity, he usually assumes that the human beings who produce, exchange, and consume, are actuated by no other motive than that of securing, under a *régime* of free competition, as large a share as possible of this wealth for themselves.

The politician, on the other hand, who has to decide what course should be pursued, not in the abstract world of science but in the concrete world of fact, cannot so limit his views. He has to provide, in so far as in him lies, for the spiritual and material well-being of the real human being, not of the imaginary wealth producer and wealth consumer which science is obliged to assume ; and knowing this, knowing that man does not live by bread alone, but is a creature of infinite variety living in a most complicated world, he can seldom decide any practical problem on purely economic grounds.

So far I have been occupied in conveying a not unneeded warning to those who, like myself, accept (speaking generally) the teaching of political economy : let me, in conclusion, make an even more earnest appeal to those who repudiate its lessons. They are to be found, not merely among those who are repelled by the difficulties and technicalities of the study ; not merely among those who — confident in what they call their practical knowledge—that is, their knowledge of the details necessary for the conduct of their own particular business—are contemptuous of all speculation ; not merely among those who dislike

the theory because, on purely selfish grounds, they
first dislike the conclusions which rightly or wrongly
are based upon it; but among those who are most
zealous and most disinterested in their efforts for the
general welfare. Burning with a desire to remedy
the ills they see on every side, these philanthropists
are impatient of a science which is apt to beget a wise
if chilling scepticism as to the efficacy of short cuts
to universal happiness. Eager to employ in the
redress of wrongs the most powerful machinery at
their disposal, viz. that of State interference, they
resent the criticism to which political economy has
subjected the grounds on which plan after plan of
State interference has been recommended to the
public. Glowing themselves with a generous enthusiasm, they are repelled, partly by the hypothesis
of universal selfishness on which political economy
for reasons to which I have already adverted appears
to proceed, partly by the cold and unfeeling manner
in which science dissects and analyses facts, warm and
palpitating with the hopes, fears, and sufferings of a
whole civilisation. That these prejudices, though
partly justified by errors of treatment on the part of
political economists, rest in the main upon a mere

confusion of thought whose nature I have already indicated, I need not stop to prove. It is only necessary to say a word on the evils they are likely to produce. I am not here to advocate any particular system of economic doctrine. There is no question concerning either the method or the results of political economy which I for one am not prepared to consider open, provided the critic can show that he really understands the doctrine he is attacking, and is not, as commonly happens, merely laying hold of some incautious expression of Ricardo, or Mill, or whoever it may be, and laboriously refuting what never was, or has long ceased to be, a received opinion. I plead not for any special scientific doctrine, but for the application to social phenomena of scientific methods. Nor has there ever been a time when, in my judgment, this was more required than it is now. Society is becoming more and more sensitive to the evils which exist in its midst ; more and more impatient of their continued existence. In itself this is wholly good ; but, in order that good may come of it, it behoves us to walk warily. It is, no doubt, better for us to apply appropriate remedies to our diseases than to put our whole trust in the healing powers of nature. But it is better to put our trust in the healing powers of nature than to poison ourselves straight off by swallowing the contents of the first phial presented to us by any self-constituted physician. And such self-constituted physicians are about and in large numbers—gentlemen who think that they pay Providence a compliment by assuming that for every social ill there is a speedy and effectual specific lying to hand; who regard it as impious to believe that there may be chronic diseases of the body politic as well as of any other body, or that Heaven will not hasten to bless the first heroic remedy which it pleases them in their ignorance to apply. It is true that without enthusiasm nothing will be done. But it is also true that without knowledge nothing will be done well. Philanthropic zeal supplies admirable motive power, but makes a very indifferent compass; and of two evils it is better, perhaps, that our ship shall go nowhere than that it shall go wrong, that it should stand still than that it should run upon the rocks. As, therefore, nature knows nothing of good intentions, rewarding and punishing not motives but actions; as things are what they are, describe them as we may, and their consequences will be what they will be, prophesy of them as we choose; it behoves us at this time of all others to approach the consideration of impending social questions in the spirit of scientific inquiry, and to be impartial investigators of social facts before we become zealous reformers of social wrongs.

VI

A FRAGMENT ON PROGRESS [1]

THERE is no more interesting characteristic of ordinary social and political speculation than the settled belief that there exists a natural law or tendency governing human affairs by which, on the whole, and in the long run, the general progress of our race is ensured. I do not know that any very precise view is entertained as to the nature of this law or tendency, its mode of operation, or its probable limits; but it is understood to be established, or at least indicated, by the general course of History, and to be in harmony with modern developments of the doctrine of Evolution.

The argument from History usually presents itself somewhat in this form. Man, it is said, has

---

[1] Lord Rector's Address, delivered at Glasgow University, November 26, 1891.

R

been working out his destiny through countless
generations, and from the first epoch of which
any record has survived, down to our own day,
his course, though subject to many mutations, has,
in the main, been one of steady and enormous
improvement. Fix your eyes, indeed, upon one
race, or one age, and you may have to admit that
there have been long periods during which there
has been no movement, or a movement only of
retrogression. But the torpor that has paralysed
one branch of the human family has been balanced
by the youthful vigour of another; now one nation,
and now another, may have led the van, but the van
itself has been ever pressing forward; and though
there have been periods in the world's history
when it may well have seemed to the most sanguine
observers that the powers that make for progress
were exhausted, that culture was giving place to
barbarism, and civil order to unlettered anarchy,
time and the event have shown that such prophets
were wrong, and out of the wreck of the old order
a new order has always arisen more perfect and
more full of promise than that which it replaced.

The argument seems seductive; yet in the

absence of any established law underlying this empirical generalisation, it has after all but little value. For the same facts can without difficulty be stated so as to suggest precisely the opposite conclusion. A survey of the world, it may be replied, shows us a vast number of savage communities, apparently at a stage of culture not profoundly different from that which prevailed among prehistoric man during geological epochs which, estimated by any historical standard, are immensely remote. History, again, tells us of successive civilisations which have been born, have for a space thriven exceedingly, and have then miserably perished. And as it shows us samples of death and decay, so it shows us samples of growth arrested, and, as far as we can tell, permanently arrested, at some particular stage of development. What is there in all this to indicate that a nation or group of nations, which happens to be under observation during its period of energetic growth, is either itself to be an exception to this common law, or is of necessity to find in some other race an heir fitted for the task of carrying on its work? Progressive civilisation is no form of indestructible energy which, if repressed

here must needs break out there, if refused embodiment in one shape must needs show itself in another.
It is a plant of tender habit, difficult to propagate,
not difficult to destroy, that refuses to flourish except
in a soil which is not to be found everywhere, nor
at all times, nor even, so far as we can see, necessarily to be found at all.

I conceive, therefore, that those who look forward
to a period of continuous and, so to speak, *inevitable*
progress, are bound to assign some more solid reason
for their convictions than a merely empirical survey
of the surface lessons of history. They must find
some tendencies deep-rooted in the nature of things
which may be trusted gradually to work out the
desired result. And this, to do them justice, they
have not been slow to attempt. Two such causes, or
groups of causes, have been assigned which deserve
special consideration, the one eminently characteristic of the second half of the nineteenth century, the
other not less characteristic of the latter half of the
eighteenth. The former, or biological, relies on the
gradual improvement both of the human and of the
social organism through the continued operation of
those laws by which evolution in general has been

effected. The latter relies on the spread of enlightenment, the dissipation of prejudice, the conscious
application to social problems of unfettered criticism,
the deliberate reconstruction of the whole social fabric
upon rational principles. These two theories are not,
of course, mutually exclusive; since, for example, no
evolutionist would deny that the intentional adaptation of institutions to foreseen results must play a
part—possibly a large part—in the development of a
social and rational animal. Nevertheless, the two
ways of estimating the history of the past and
attacking the problem of the future, differ profoundly
both in the letter and in the spirit, and they require,
therefore, separate treatment at our hands.

Now, no one, I conceive, will be found to-day
anxious to dispute the proposition that the same laws
which have operated in the organic world of animals
and plants may have had much, and must have had
something, to do with moulding the destiny of man.
In dealing with the causes which ages before the
dawn of history produced the various physical and
mental qualities of the different races of the world,
we are no doubt necessarily reduced to dim conjecture. But we can hardly be wrong in supposing

that, during the vast period in which a blind struggle
with the forces of nature and with each other, was
the main occupation of men, and when defeat in either
contest meant death, the weeding out of unfit individuals and unfit institutions was an active agency
in shaping the characteristics of humanity, as it still
is in shaping those of the lower animals. We may
conceive without difficulty, indeed we can hardly
refuse to believe that the "natural man"—man (that
is) as he is born into the world as distinguished from
man as he afterwards makes himself and is made by
his surroundings, might thus by elimination and
selection undergo a process of profound modification ;
that in dexterity of muscle and, still more, in power
of brain an enormous improvement might easily take
place ; and even that special aptitudes for social life,
involving, of course, an innate predisposition to accept
a morality without which social life is impossible,
might be bred into the physical organisation of the
most successful races. But this particular cause of
progress has, we can scarcely doubt, lost most of its
strength. Nay, if certain theorists are right, and it
requires the unsparing slaughter of all the inferior
members of a species to maintain its effectiveness at

its normal level,—to preserve the speed of the antelope undiminished and the sight of the eagle undimmed,— then we can hardly refuse our support to the view that the general improvement of the race may in some respects lead to a deterioration in the natural constitution of the individual. Humanity, civilisation, progress itself, must have a tendency to mitigate the harsh methods by which Nature has wrought out the variety and the perfection of organic life. And however much man as he is ultimately moulded by the social forces surrounding him may gain, man as he is born into the world must somewhat lose; the loss in the quality of the raw material being thus a deduction, it may be even a large deduction, to be set off against the advantages obtained by better processes of manufacture.

It has, however, been thought by many that there are biological causes at work which may compensate, and more than compensate, the kind of loss produced by the greatly diminished efficiency of elimination and selection. The majority of naturalists have held, and I suppose still hold, that modifications in the physical structure of animals produced during life may be transmitted to their offspring, and that by the cumulative effect of such changes, profound alterations may gradually be made in the characteristics of a species. And there is one systematic philosopher[1] of our own day who has applied this principle so persistently in every department of his theory of Man, that were it to be upset, it is scarcely too much to say that his Ethics, his Psychology, and his Anthropology would all tumble to the ground with it. Yet this doctrine has for many years been questioned by a great English authority,[2] and, as many of you are aware, it has been directly controverted by one of the most eminent living German biologists. This is not the occasion, and assuredly I am not the person, to attempt to sum up the argument or to pronounce upon the merits of this interesting controversy. For my present purpose it will be enough if I remind you that Weisman's conclusions are largely based on the extreme difficulty of conceiving any possible theory of heredity by which the transmission of acquired qualities could be accounted for; on the relative simplicity and plausibility of his own theory of heredity, according to which the transmission would be impossible; and on the absence

[1] Mr. Herbert Spencer.   [2] Mr. F. Galton.

of any conclusive proof that the transmission has ever taken place. It may no doubt be objected (I do not say rightly objected) to such a line of argument, that even the simplest explanations of heredity are so mysterious, and involve so large an element of unverifiable hypothesis, that it is rash to lay too much stress on the difference in these respects which may exist between one speculation and another ; that evidence from experience cannot at most be said to prove more than that many qualities patiently acquired by generation after generation do not seem, as a matter of fact, to have become hereditary ; while as a matter of theory, qualities which are undoubtedly hereditary can seldom if ever be shown to have been originally acquired.

I cannot but think, however, that even in this qualified form the lessons to be learned from the discussion are full of interest from our present point of view. We have got into the habit of thinking that the efforts at progress made by each generation may not only bear fruit for succeeding ones, in the growth of knowledge, the bettering of habits and institutions, and the increase of wealth, but that there may also be a process, so to speak, of *physio-*

logical accumulation, by which the dexterities painfully learned by the fathers shall descend as inherited aptitudes to the sons, and not merely the manufactured man—man as he makes himself and is made by his surroundings,—but the natural man also, may thus go through a course of steady and continuous improvement. It now seems, I think, probable, that not in this more than in other cases is biology necessarily optimist. For as it has long been known that the causes by which species have been modified are not inconsistent with an immobility of type lasting through geological epochs; as it is also known that these causes may lead to what we call deterioration as well as to what we call improvement; as it is impossible to believe that selection and elimination can play any very important part in the further development of civilised man; so now the gravest doubts have been raised as to whether there are any other physiological causes in operation by which that development is likely to be secured.

If this be so we must regard the raw material, as I have called it, of civilisation as being now, in all probability, at its best, and henceforth for the amelioration of mankind we must look to the perfec-

tion of manufacture. But do not let any one suppose
that the possible results of manufacture are insignificant. Doubtless they are strictly conditioned by
the quality of the stuff that has to be worked on.
Doubtless this quality differs essentially in each of
the great families of mankind. They have emerged
from the dim workshop where the rough machinery
of nature has, in remotest ages, wrought into each
its inalienable heritage of natural gifts and aptitudes;
—and by these must the character and limits of
their development in part be determined. But let
us not found more upon this truth than it will bear.
In our social and political speculations we are surely
apt to think too much of ethnology, and too little
of history. Sometimes from a kind of idleness,
sometimes from a kind of pride, sometimes because
the "principles of heredity" is now always on our
lips, we frequently attribute to differences of blood
effects which are really due to differences of surroundings. We note, and note correctly, the varying
shades of national character; and proceed to put
them down, often most incorrectly, to variations in
national descent. The population of one district is
Teutonic, and therefore it does this; the population

of the other district is Celtic, and therefore it does that. A Jewish strain explains one peculiarity; a Greek strain explains another; and so on. Conjectures like these appear to be of the most dubious value. We know by experience that a nation may suddenly blaze out into a splendour of productive genius, of which its previous history gave but faint promise, and of which its subsequent history shows but little trace; some great crisis in its fate may stamp upon a race marks which neither lapse of time nor change of circumstance seem able wholly to efface; and empires may rise from barbarism to civilisation and sink again from civilisation into barbarism, within periods so brief that we may take it as certain, whatever be our opinion as to the transmission of acquired faculties, that no hereditary influence has had time to operate. Now, if the differences between the same nation at different times are thus obviously not due to differences in inherited qualities, is it not somewhat rash to drag in hypothetical differences in inherited qualities to account for the often slighter peculiarities of temperament by which communities of different descent may be distinguished? Are we not often attributing to heredity what is properly due to education, and crediting Nature with what really is the work of Man?

So far, then, we have arrived at the double conclusion that, while there is, to say the least, no sufficient ground for expecting that our descendants will be provided by Nature with better "organisms" than our own, it is nevertheless not impossible to suppose that they may be able to provide themselves with a much more commodious "environment." And this is not on the face of it wholly unsatisfactory; for if, on the one hand, it seems to forbid us to indulge in visions of a millennium in which there shall not only be a new heaven and a new earth, but also a new variety of the human race to enjoy them; on the other hand it permits us to hope that the efforts of successive generations may so improve the surroundings into which men are born that the community of the far future may be as much superior to us as we are to our barbarian ancestors.

Our expectations, however, that any such hope will be realised must depend largely on the efficiency which we are justified in attributing to the "efforts of successive generations"—must depend, in other words, on the value we are disposed to attach to the

second or "rational" theory of progress which I mentioned earlier in this paper. This theory assumes
that every community, at least every self-governing
community, holds its fate in its hands, and is itself
the intelligent arbiter of its own destiny. Its efforts
may be as immediately and as effectively directed to
the work of promoting progress as the efforts of a
navvy to the work of raising a weight. What is to
be done is clear; how to do it may easily be discovered:
nothing more, therefore, is required to attain success
but strenuous and single-minded endeavour. Unfortunately the world is not made on so simple a plan,
nor is the problem to be dealt with one in elementary mechanics : so complex is it indeed that I
could not attempt on such an occasion even roughly to
formulate it in its entirety. But the most cursory
observation will show that in many cases endeavour is
not enough, even when endeavour is made. Consider,
for instance, the case of Art. Mr. Spencer cherishes
the belief that his "fully evolved" man will spend much
more time in æsthetic enjoyment than our toil-worn
generation is permitted to do. I hope he may. But
what art is he going to enjoy ? Leisure and fashion
will produce audiences and spectators. We know of

nothing that will produce musicians or painters : and I sometimes fear that if Mr. Spencer's "fully evolved man" ever comes into being, he will not only find perfect "harmony with his environment" intolerably tedious, but will be in the humiliating position of having to depend for his higher pleasures on the Poetry and Painting of his "imperfectly evolved" forefathers, whose harmony with their environment was, perhaps, fortunately for the cause of Art, not quite so perfect as his own.

Consider, again, the case of Knowledge. Growth in Knowledge, like productiveness in Art, can hardly, so far as its direct consequences are concerned, do otherwise than subserve the cause of progress. But, unlike productiveness in Art, it would seem to be under some kind of control. It is true, no doubt, that the greatest achievements in discovery, like the greatest creations of the imagination, depend largely upon individual genius ;—depend, that is, upon something which is, and which will probably remain, wholly accidental and incalculable. Nevertheless a community which, individually or collectively, was sufficiently interested in the matter, might apparently be as certain of having an annual output of scientific research and industrial invention, as a farmer is of growing an annual crop of wheat or barley; and, within limits, this is probably the fact. I would only note that the presupposed appetite for scientific knowledge and the demand for industrial invention, have been rare in the history of the world; that advanced civilisations have existed without them, and that we certainly do not know enough of the causes by which they have been produced to enable us to say with any assurance that they will persist in places where they are now to be found, or arise in places from which they are now absent. But granting their existence, may we assume that knowledge will grow without limit? In an age distinguished for its scientific progress, and in the presence of some by whom that progress has been largely promoted, I scarcely dare suggest a doubt on such a question. Indeed, with regard to one aspect of it, I feel no doubt. Unquestionably mankind will be able to cultivate the field of scientific discovery to all time without exhausting it. But is it so certain that they will be able indefinitely to extend it? Industrial invention need never cease. But will our general theory of the material Universe again undergo any revolution comparable to that which it has undergone in the last four hundred years? It is at least uncertain. We seem indeed even at this moment to stand on the verge of some great co-ordination of the energies of nature, and to be perhaps within a measurable distance of comprehending the cause of gravitation and the character of that ethereal medium which is the vehicle of Light, Magnetism, and Electricity. Yet though this be true, it is also true that in whatever direction we drive our explorations we come upon limits we cannot, as it seems to me, hope to overpass. Consider, for example, the case of Astronomy—the region of investigation in which the results already obtained are, perhaps, in some respects the most unexpected and the most impressive. Far-reaching as they seem, the theories dealing with the constitution, movements, and evolution of the heavenly bodies, are all, without exception, ultimately based upon terrestrial analogies and upon laws of which in some of their manifestations we have terrestrial experience. If these fail us, we are, and must remain, perfectly helpless. Supposing it to be true, for instance, that the proper motion of the stars cannot in many cases be reasonably attributed to gravitation. Does it not seem almost certain that we are here in presence of a force on which we can never experiment, and whose laws we shall never be able to determine? Again, in Physics, the admirable results which have been attained, blind us sometimes to the fact that where we have been successful has been in the case of phenomena which, though in their reality they can never be directly perceived, are nevertheless analogous to objects of sensible experience, which can therefore be readily if not adequately imagined, and about which hypotheses can be made simple enough to be treated mathematically. No man will ever see what goes on in a gas, or know by direct vision how ether behaves. But we can all of us think of a collision or a vibration, and a few of us can deal with them by calculation. But observe how rapidly the difficulty of comprehension increases as soon as sensible analogies begin to fail, as they do in the case of many electric and magnetic phenomena; and how quickly the difficulty becomes an impossibility when, as in the case of the most important organic processes, the operations to be observed are too minute ever to be seen and too complex ever to be calculated. It is no imperfection in our instruments which here foils us. It is an incurable imperfection

in ourselves. Our senses are very few and very imperfect. They were not, unfortunately, evolved for
purposes of research. And though we may well
stand amazed at the immense scientific structure
which Mankind have been able to raise on the meagre
foundations afforded by their feeble sense-perceptions,
we can hardly hope to see it added to without limit.
Nor is the time necessarily as far distant as we sometimes think, when we may be reduced either to
elaborating the details of that which in outline is
known already, or to framing dim conjectures about
that which cannot scientifically be known at all.

These passing doubts, however, as to the future
triumphs of Art and Science, be they well or ill
founded, need not, it may be said, affect our estimate
of the results which in other departments of human
activity may be expected to flow from the " efforts of
successive generations," made through the machinery
by which alone in its *collective* capacity the community
can make a deliberate attempt at progress—I mean
the State. It is unnecessary to remind you what
immense expectations have been, and are, based upon
State action. We are all familiar with that numerous class who see in political changes the main interest

of the Past, and their main hopes for the Future; who, if asked what they mean by Progress, will tell you Reform; and if asked what they mean by Reform, will tell you, "An alteration of the State Constitution," and if asked why they desire an alteration of the State Constitution, will tell you, "In order to carry on more rapidly and effectively the work of Progress."

For this view ordinary History is, no doubt, partly responsible. Such history is largely employed in giving an account of the mode in which political institutions have from time to time been modified to suit the changing wishes or the changing needs of the community, or of some portion of it. It is full of accounts of violent and often sanguinary disputes, in the decision of which the two sides held at the time, and the historian has held after them, that the most important interests of the community were involved. Yet, if this proposition is true at all, it is certainly not true in the sense in which it is commonly accepted. Consider, for instance, how different has been the political history, and yet how similar is the social condition, of Great Britain, France, Germany, Holland, and Belgium. Though these five nations do not for the most part speak the same language, nor profess the same religion, nor claim the same ancestry; though the events by which they have been moulded, and the institutions by which they have been governed, are apparently widely dissimilar; yet their culture is at this moment practically identical; their ideas form a common stock; the social questions they have to face are the same; and such differences as exist in the material condition and wellbeing of their populations are unquestionably due more to the economic differences in their position, climate, and natural advantages, than to the decisions at which they may have from time to time arrived on the various political controversies by which their peoples have been so bitterly divided. We cannot, of course, conclude from this that political action or inaction has no effect upon the broad stream of human progress; still less that it may not largely determine for good or for evil the course of its smaller eddies and subsidiary currents. All that we are warranted in saying is that, as a matter of fact, the differences in the political history of these five communities, however interesting to the historian, nay, however important at the moment to the happiness of the populations concerned, are, if estimated by the scale we are at this moment applying to human affairs, almost negligible; and that it must be in connection with the points wherein their political systems agree that the importance of those systems is principally to be found.

Nor need this conclusion seem strange or paradoxical. For great as are the recent changes which have taken place in Western civilisation, they have been almost entirely due to scientific discoveries, to industrial inventions, to commercial enterprise, to the occupation by Europeans of new Continents, to the slow and in the main consequential modification of our beliefs, ideas, and governing conceptions. But to these great causes of movement the State, in the cases to which I have referred, has contributed little but the external conditions under which individual effort has been able to operate unhindered—conditions consisting for the most part in a tolerable degree of security, and a tolerable degree of freedom; and the great political movements with which the historian chiefly concerns himself must be regarded as symptoms, rather than as causes, of the vital changes which have taken place.

I hold, then, that the actual uses to which political action within the community has been, and is being, put are in the main rather negative than positive. Such action does not to any great extent supply the causes which advance the world, it only provides the conditions under which the world may be advanced. Even those, however, who agree with this estimate of what in fact has commonly happened in the recent past, might hold, and in many cases do hold, that much more than this may be made to happen in the future. It is admitted, they might say, that the destiny of each generation is, to an almost incalculable degree, determined by the social conditions in the midst of which it is born. It is admitted that these conditions are principally the handiwork of man himself. It is admitted that no instrument at our command is more powerful than the collective action of the community. Why not, then, employ it to create the environment by which the progress we desire may be hastened and ensured?

Now to answer this question we must know both whether the community whose intervention is invoked has the requisite knowledge, and whether, if so, it has also the power to turn this knowledge to account.

It is curious that the first of these problems hardly seems to have presented itself to whole schools of political thinkers who flourished at the end of the last century, and the beginning of this. According to their view, an acquaintance with the "Law of Nature" was enough, and the "Law of Nature" could be understood by all who brought to its study an unprejudiced mind. This remarkable doctrine even now survives to an astonishing extent; and there are still plenty of excellent gentlemen who appear to be exclusively preoccupied with the task of making the opinion of the community, or what passes for such, act rapidly and effectively on the administrative machine; never supposing, apparently, that if it could be made to act rapidly and effectively there could be any doubts as to what it ought to do. And yet there is no sign that sociology, or even the limited department of it concerned with politics, exists or ever will exist except in the shape of a certain number of valuable empirical maxims, and a few very wide and not very trustworthy generalisations. The science has been planned out by some very able philosophers, much as a prospective watering-place is planned out by a speculative builder. But the streets, the squares, the theatres, and the piers of this scientific city have so far no existence except in

imagination—nor are they likely soon to be constructed.   Much indeed of what commonly figures
as the theory of Politics has nothing, properly
speaking, to do with Sociology at all.   The whole
tribe of Utopias; the innumerable theories deduced
from the abstract rights or moral obligations of
individuals or communities; all speculations which
concern themselves, not with explaining what *is*, but
with telling us what *ought to be*, are, however admirable and useful, wholly alien to Science in the sense
in which that word is here used.   Such speculations
have had, and are having, for good and for evil,
important political effects; they are therefore among
the phenomena which political science must co-
ordinate and explain : but they are no more contributions to that science than an earthquake is a
contribution to Geology.

Other investigations, commonly and not incorrectly
considered as contributions to Political Knowledge,
such as those which deal with Constitutional History
and Constitutional Law, stand in a different category.
Their business is to discover and classify political facts
of great significance and interest.   They ought, therefore, it would seem, to be valuable preliminaries to

the construction of a Science of Politics.   Yet, as they are usually conducted, it may be doubted whether they do not obscure rather than illustrate its problems. They bring into undue prominence certain kinds of fact; they wholly ignore other kinds of fact at least as material to a true understanding of the real play of social laws.   For them the legal and theoretical attributes of each organ in the body politic, the forms and fictions of exoteric politics, are the main subjects of interest, and supply the only principles of classification; while the ever-varying social forces which successively work through the same constitutional mechanism, and which give to the latter its chief significance, are comparatively neglected.   That this should be so is perhaps inevitable.   For while it is easy, with the lawyers, to analyse the documents, or the precedents on which are based the legal and constitutional powers of every governing element in a State; while it is not difficult, with the historians, to trace the formal growth and gradual transformation of these various elements through successive generations, the difficulty of any systematic inquiry into the essential sequences of social phenomena are great, and perhaps on any large scale insuperable.   We are apt to be

misled in this matter by a false scientific analogy.
We often talk, and sometimes think, as if its political
constitution was to the State what its anatomical con-
formation is to the living animal : and as if therefore
we might argue from " structure " to " function " with
the same degree of assurance in the one case as we
habitually do in the other.   But there is little
analogy between the two.   The trite comparison
between a community and an organism is doubtless
suggestive, and may be useful.   But it can only be
employed in security by those who remember that
among the organs through which the vital energies
of society act, and by which they are conditioned,
those whose character is described in constitutional
text-books, and whose growth is traced in constitutional histories, are among the least interesting, and
the least important.

If I desired to illustrate the consequences which
follow upon forgetfulness of these truths, I might
remind you of the absurd controversies, dear to the
debating societies of two generations ago, and not
perhaps quite forgotten in some political clubs even
now, on the relative merits of various abstract forms
of government—Monarchical, Republican, Aristocratic,

Democratic, and so forth.   But let me take a less crude form of the same kind of error.   We are all of us prone to regard a political institution, for instance, a representative chamber, as a machine whose character can be adequately expressed by defining its legal constitution.   When we have mastered this, when we know the qualification of its electors, its legislative powers, its relation to other bodies in the State, and so forth, we conceive ourselves to have mastered its theory, and to be qualified to pronounce an opinion on the way it will work in practice.   But, in truth, we have only mastered a certain modicum of constitutional law ; and Constitutional law may (as I have said), be in some respects, an obstacle rather than an aid, to the construction of Political Science.   The second is concerned with the reality of things, the first with their form.   The subject-matter of one is Natural law, of the other Statute law.   The assumed line between the theory of the political machine and its practical working, either cannot be drawn at all, or cannot be drawn at the place where legal definition and enactment end.   No statute, for example, provides or could provide that a popular assembly shall work through a few large and well-disciplined parties, rather than through a number of small and independent groups.   Yet its habits in this respect are incomparably more important than anything in its formal constitution.   No statute provides or could provide that the representatives composing it shall, on the whole, be elected from among those who do not regard politics as a means of making money. Yet the habits of the electorate in this respect are incomparably more important than any mere question of the franchise.   On the other hand, the constitution of most representative assemblies does assume that the units who elect and the units who are elected shall, as among themselves, possess equal fractions of political power : and, accordingly, the law is careful to draw no distinction between them.   But here, again, Law is no guide to fact.   Legal equality has no necessary connection with political equivalence, and the most cursory observations, not of constitutional forms, but of the realities of life, show that organisation is the inevitable accompaniment of electoral institutions, and that organisation, from the very nature of the case, is absolutely incompatible with uniformity.

All this goes to show that we are not yet in

possession of anything deserving the name of political science; that the intrinsic difficulties of creating one are almost insurmountable; and that in most cases those who attempt the task employ methods essentially arbitrary, and predestined from the beginning to be unfruitful. But though it may well seem doubtful whether a complete science of politics (and *a fortiori* of sociology) will ever exist, it is quite certain that if it ever does exist it must be confined to a small body of experts. Is there the slightest probability that in their hands it could ever produce the practical results which many persons hope for? It may be doubted. An acquaintance with the laws of nature does not always, nor even commonly, carry with it the means of controlling them. Knowledge is seldom power. And a sociologist so coldly independent of the social forces among which he lived as thoroughly to understand them, would, in all probability, be as impotent to guide the evolution of a community as an astronomer to modify the orbit of a comet.

It might indeed at first sight appear that while the astronomer has no means of intervening in the affairs of the star, it is always open to the sociologist

to appeal to the reason of the community of which
he is a member. But this view depends, I think,
on an erroneous view of the influence which reasoning has or can have on the course of human affairs.
To hear some people talk, one would suppose that
the successful working of social institutions depended
as much upon cool calculation as the management
of a Joint Stock Bank: that from top to bottom,
and side to side, it was a mere question of political
arithmetic; and that the beliefs, the affections, the
passions and the prejudices of Mankind were to be
considered in no other light than as obstacles in the
path of progress, which it was the business of the politician to destroy or to elude. This is a natural and,
perhaps in some respects, a beneficial illusion. Movement, whether of progress or of retrogression, can
commonly be brought about only when the sentiments
opposing it have been designedly weakened or have
suffered a natural decay. In this destructive process,
and in any constructive process by which it may be
followed, reasoning, often very bad reasoning, bears,
at least in Western communities, a large share as cause,
a still larger share as symptom; so that the clatter of
contending argumentation is often the most striking

accompaniment of interesting social changes. Its position, therefore, and its functions in the social organism,
are frequently misunderstood. People fall instinctively
into the habit of supposing that, as it plays a con-
spicuous part in the improvement or deterioration of
human institutions, it therefore supplies the very basis
on which they may be made to rest, the very mould to
which they ought to conform ; and they naturally conclude that we have only got to reason more and to
reason better, in order speedily to perfect the whole
machinery by which human felicity is to be secured.

Surely this is a great delusion. A community
founded upon argument would soon be a community
no longer. It would dissolve into its constituent
elements. Think of the thousand ties most subtly
woven out of common sentiments, common tastes,
common beliefs, nay, common prejudices, by which
from our very earliest childhood we are all bound
unconsciously but indissolubly together into a com-
pacted whole. Imagine these to be suddenly loosed
and their places taken by some judicious piece of
reasoning on the balance of advantage, which, after
making all proper deductions, still remains to the
credit of social life. Imagine nicely adjusting our

loyalty and our patriotism to the standard of a
calculated utility. Imagine us severally suspending
our adhesion to the Ten Commandments until we have
leisure and opportunity to decide between the rival
and inconsistent philosophies which contend for the
honour of establishing them! These things we may
indeed imagine if we please. Fortunately, we shall
never see them. Society is founded—and from the
nature of the human beings which constitute it, must,
in the main, be always founded—not upon criticism
but upon feelings and beliefs, and upon the customs
and codes by which feelings and beliefs are, as it were,
fixed and rendered stable. And even where these
harmonise so far as we can judge with sound reason,
they are in many cases not consciously based on
reasoning; nor is their fate necessarily bound up with
that of the extremely indifferent arguments by which,
from time to time, philosophers, politicians, and I
will add divines, have thought fit to support them.

This view may, perhaps, be readily accepted in
reference, for instance, to Oriental civilisation; but
to some it may seem paradoxical when applied to the
free constitutions of the West. Yet, after all, it
supplies the only possible justification, I will not say

T

for Democratic Government only, but for any Government whatever based on public opinion. If the business of such a Government was to deal with the essential framework of society as an engineer deals with the wood and iron out of which he constructs a bridge, it would be as idiotic to govern by household suffrage as to design the Forth Bridge by household suffrage. Indeed, it would be much more idiotic, because, as we have seen, sociology is far more difficult than engineering. But, in truth, there is no resemblance between the two cases. We habitually talk as if a self-governing or free community was one which managed its own affairs. In strictness, no community manages its own affairs, or by any possibility could manage them. It manages but a narrow fringe of its affairs, and that in the main by deputy. It is only the thinnest surface layer of law and custom, belief and sentiment, which can either be successfully subjected to destructive treatment, or become the nucleus of any new growth—a fact which explains the apparent paradox that so many of our most famous advances in political wisdom are nothing more than the formal recognition of our political impotence.

Examples of this paradox from the history of economic legislation will at once suggest themselves to all. But consider an illustration which in this connection may not seem so familiar, drawn from the theory of toleration.

As we are all aware, this theory was never accepted, unless now and then by the persecuted minority, until quite recent times. It is doubtless one of the most valuable empirical maxims of modern politics. Yet the reasons given for it are usually bad. Some will tell you, oblivious of the most patent facts of history, that persecution is always unsuccessful. Others appear to assume that there is an inherent and inalienable right possessed by every human being to hold and to propagate what opinions he pleases—a doctrine which cannot be held practically in an absolute form, or logically in a limited one. Others again, with more reason, point out that the persecutor never can be quite sure he is right; that new truths have constantly been unpopular in their first beginnings; and that if every modification of received beliefs or customs is to be destroyed as soon as it is born, progress becomes impossible.

This is all very true. But it is far from going to

the root of the matter.   Persecution is only an
attempt to do that overtly and with violence, which
the community is, in self-defence, perpetually doing
unconsciously and in silence.   In many societies
variation of belief is practically impossible.   In other
societies it is permitted only along certain definite
lines.   In no society that has ever existed, or could
be conceived as existing, are opinions equally free (in
the *scientific* sense of the term, not the *legal*) to develop
themselves indifferently in all directions.   The constant pressure of custom; the effects of imitation, of
education, and of habit; the incalculable influence of
man on man, produce a working uniformity of conviction more effectually than the gallows and the
stake, though without the cruelty, and with far more
than the wisdom that have usually been vouchsafed
to official persecutors.   Though the production of
such a community of ideas as is necessary to make
possible community of life, the encouragement of
useful novelties, the destruction of dangerous eccen-
tricities, are thus among the undertakings which,
according to modern notions, the State dare scarcely
touch, or touches not at all, this is not because these
things are unimportant, but because, though among

the most important of our affairs, we no longer think we can manage them.

It would seem, then, that in all States, and not least in those which are loosely described as self-governing, the governmental action which can ever be truly described as the conscious application of appropriate means to the attainment of fully-comprehended ends, must, in comparison with the totality of causes affecting the development of the community, be extremely insignificant in amount. As a matter of fact, it has, in the recent past, been in the main confined to questions of administration and finance, or to the removal, sometimes, no doubt, by revolutionary means, of antiquated and vexatious restrictions. Far more than this may, of course, be attempted. It is quite possible to conceive an absolute government with a taste for social experiments. It is quite possible, though not so easy, to conceive a popular government in which the strength of custom and tradition shall have been seriously weakened by criticism or other causes, and where the sentiments which usually support what *is*, begin, by a kind of inverted conservatism, to nourish and give strength to some ideal of what *ought to be*. Communities so situated are in a condition of unstable equilibrium.   They are in danger of far-reaching changes.   It is not asserted that the result of such changes must be unsuccessful, only that it is beyond our powers of calculation.   The new condition of things would be a political parallel to what breeders and biologists call in natural history a "sport."   Such "sports" do not often survive; still less often do they flourish and multiply.   It can only be by a rare and happy accident that either in the social or the physical world they constitute a stable and permanent variety.

We are therefore driven to the conclusion that, as our expectations of limitless progress for the race cannot depend upon the blind operation of the laws of heredity, so neither can they depend upon the deliberate action of national governments.   Such examination as we can make of the changes which have taken place during the relatively minute fraction of history with respect to which we have fairly full information, shows that they have been caused by a multitude of variations, often extremely small, made in their surroundings by individuals whose objects, though not necessarily selfish, have often had no intentional reference to the advancement of the community at large. But we have no scientific ground for suspecting that the stimulus to these individual efforts must necessarily continue ; we know of no law by which, if they do continue, they must needs be co-ordinated for a common purpose or pressed into the service of the common good. We cannot estimate their remoter consequences ; neither can we tell how they will act and re-act upon one another, nor how they will in the long run affect morality, religion, and other fundamental elements of human society. The future of the race is thus encompassed with darkness : no faculty of calculation that we possess, no instrument that we are likely to invent, will enable us to map out its course, or penetrate the secret of its destiny. It is easy, no doubt, to find in the clouds which obscure our path what shapes we please : to see in them the promise of some millennial paradise, or the threat of endless and unmeaning travel through waste and perilous places. But in such visions the wise man will put but little confidence : content, in a sober and cautious spirit, with a full consciousness of his feeble powers of foresight, and the narrow limits of his activity, to deal as they arise with the problems of his own generation.

In thinking over the criticisms which this hasty survey of an immense subject might possibly provoke, two in particular seem to require some special notice on my part. To the first I plead guilty at once. It will be objected that of many statements the proof is not given at all, or is but barely indicated; that no notice has been taken of many obvious objections, and that the treatment of the most important topics has been so meagre that what I have said rather resembles the syllabus of a course of lectures than a lecture complete in itself. All this is perfectly true; and I can only urge in palliation that, as I could not deliver a series of Rectorial Addresses, what I had to say must either have been compressed, as I have endeavoured to compress it, or not be said at all; and further, that I had the good fortune to speak to an audience who might be trusted to fill up the *lacunæ* which I had been compelled to leave.

The second criticism is of a different kind, and to this I do *not* plead guilty. I shall be told, indeed I have already been told, that the treatment of the subject was unsuited to the occasion, and to the age of many among my audience ; that it was calculated to chill youthful enthusiasm, and to check youthful enterprise. Now I quite agree that it would be a melancholy result of our meeting if any single member of this assembly left it with a lower view of the intrinsic worth of human endeavour. But I do not believe this is likely to be the case. It is true that, as I think, there is nothing in what we know of the earthly prospects of humanity fitted fully to satisfy human aspirations. It is true that, as I think, much optimistic speculation about the future is quite unworthy the consideration of serious men. It is true that, as I think, the light-hearted manner in which many persons sketch out their ideas of a re-constructed society exhibits an almost comic igno-rance of our limited powers of political calculation.

But I do not believe that these opinions are likely, either in reason or in fact, to weaken the springs of human effort. The best efforts of mankind have never been founded upon the belief in an assured progress towards a terrestrial millennium : if for no other reason because the belief itself is quite modern. Patriotism and public zeal have not in the past, and

do not now, require any such aliment.   True we do
not know, as our fathers before us have not known,
the hidden laws by which in any State the private
virtues of its citizens, their love of knowledge, the
energy and disinterestedness of their civic life, their
reverence for the past, their caution, their capacity
for safely working free institutions, may be maintained and fostered.   But we *do* know that no State
where these qualities have flourished has ever perished
from internal decay ; and we also know that it is
within our power, each of us in his own sphere, to
practise them ourselves, and to encourage them in
others.   As men of action, we want no more than
this.   Of this no speculation can deprive us.   And I
doubt whether any of us will be less fitted to face
with a wise and cheerful courage the problems of our
age and country, if reflection should induce us to rate
somewhat lower than is at present fashionable, either
the splendours of our future destiny, or the facility
with which these splendours may be attained.

VII

THE RELIGION OF HUMANITY[1]

THE word Positivism, as used by us to-day, I understand to carry with it no special reference to the peculiarities of Comte's system, to his views on the historic evolution of thought, to his classification of the sciences, to his theories of sociology, or to those curious schemes of polity and ritual contained in his later writings, which have tried the fidelity of his disciples and the gravity of his critics. I rather suppose the word to be used in a wider sense. I take it to mean that general habit or scheme of thought which, on its negative side, refuses all belief in anything beyond phenomena and the laws connecting them, and on its positive side attempts to find in the

[1] An Address delivered at the Church Congress, Manchester, October 1888.

"worship of humanity," or, as some more soberly phrase it, in the "service of man," a form of religion unpolluted by any element of the supernatural.

Now I do not propose here to discuss the negative side of this creed. Those who confidently assert, as do the Positivists, that there is one set of things which we can know and do know, and another set of things which we do not know and can never know, evidently suppose themselves to be in possession of some valid criterion of knowledge. How far this supposition is in their case legitimate, I have endeavoured elsewhere to discuss from my own point of view, in a book the title of which has attracted more interest than the contents. I do not mean to refer to the subject here. What I have now to say relates solely to what may be called the religious element in Positivism, and its adequacy to meet the highest needs of beings such as we are, placed in a world such as ours.

Some will deny at the outset that the term *religion* can ever be appropriately used of a creed which has nothing in it of the supernatural. It is a question of words, and, like all questions of words, a question of convenience. In my judgment the convenience varies in this case with the kind of investigation in which we happen to be engaged. If we are considering religions from their dogmatic side, as systems of belief, to be distinguished as such both from ethics and from science, no doubt it would be absurd to describe Positivism, which allows no beliefs except such as are either scientific or ethical, as having any religious element at all. So considered it is a negation of all religion. But if, on the other hand, we are considering religion not merely from the outside, as a system of propositions, stating what can be known of man's relations to a supernatural power, and the rules of conduct to be framed thereon, but from the inside, as consisting of acts of belief penetrated with religious emotion, then I think it would be unfair to deny that some such emotion may centre round the object of Positivist cult, and that if it does so it is inconvenient to refuse to describe it as a religion.

It is doubtless unnecessary for me to dwell upon this double aspect of every religion, and of every system of belief which aspires to be a substitute for religion. For many purposes it may be enough to regard religion as a mere collection of doctrines and

precepts.   It is often enough when we are dealing
with its history, or its development; with the
criticism of documents or the evidence of dogmas.
But when we are dealing not merely with the evolution of religion or its truth, but with its function
among us men here and now, we are at least as much
concerned with the living emotions of the religious
consciousness as with the framework of doctrine, on
which no doubt they ultimately depend for their
consistency and permanence.

Now, as it is certain that there may be supernaturalism without religious feeling, so we need not
deny that there may be something of the nature of
religious feeling without supernaturalism.   The Deists
of the last century accepted the argument from
design.   The existence of the world showed in their
view that there must have been a First Cause.   The
character of the world showed that this First Cause
was intelligent and benevolent.   They thus provided
themselves with the dogmatic basis of a religion,
which, however inadequate, nevertheless has been
and still is a real religion to vast numbers of men.
But to the thinkers of whom I speak this theory was
never more than a speculative belief.   The chain of

cause and effect required a beginning, and their theory of a First Cause provided one. The idea of an infinitely complex but orderly universe appeared by itself to be unsatisfactory, if not unintelligible, so they rounded it off with a God. Yet, while the savage who adores a stone, for no better reason than that it has an odd shape, possesses a religion though a wretched and degraded one, the Deists of whom I speak had nothing more than a theology, though of a kind only possible in a comparatively advanced community.

While there may thus be a speculative belief in the supernatural, which through the absence of religious feeling does not in the full sense of the word amount to a religion, there may be religious feeling divorced from any belief in the supernatural. It is indeed obvious that such feeling must be limited. To the variety and compass of the full religious consciousness it can, from the very nature of the case, never attain. The spectacle of the Starry Heavens may inspire admiration and awe, but cannot be said, except by way of metaphor, to inspire love and devotion. Humanity may inspire love and devotion, but does not, in ordinarily-constituted minds, inspire either admiration or awe. If we wish to find these and other religious feelings concentrated on one object, transfusing and vivifying the bare precepts of morality, the combining power must be sought for in the doctrines of Supernatural Religion.

It might be said in reply, that while some of the feelings associated with a supernatural theology are doubtless absent from the "religion of humanity," these have purpose and significance chiefly in relation to the doctrine of a future life, and to those persons, therefore, who see no ground for believing in the possibility of any such life, seem necessarily meaningless or mischievous. Here, then, is the point where I desire to join issue. The belief in a future state is one of the most striking—I will not say the most important — differences between positive and supernatural religion. It is one upon which no agreement or compromise is possible. It admits of no gradations—of no less or more. It is true, or it is false. And my purpose is to contribute one or two observations towards a *qualitative* estimate of the immediate gain or loss to some of the highest interests of mankind, which would follow upon a substitution of the Positivist for the Christian theory on the subject.

I say a qualitative estimate, because it is not easy to argue about a quantitative estimate in default of a kind of experience in which we are at present wholly deficient. The religion of humanity, divorced from any other religion, is professed by but a small and, in many respects, a peculiar sect. The cultivation of emotions at high tension towards humanity, deliberately dissociated from the cultivation of religious feeling towards God, has never yet been practised on a large scale. We have so far had only laboratory experiments. There has been no attempt to manufacture in bulk. And even if it had been otherwise, the conclusion to be drawn must for a long time have remained doubtful. For the success of such attempts greatly depends on the character of the social medium in which they are carried on; and if, as I should hope, the existing social medium is favourable to the growth of philanthropic feelings, its character is largely due to the action of Christianity. It remains to be proved whether, if Christianity were destroyed, a "religion of humanity" could long maintain for itself the atmosphere in which alone it could permanently flourish.

I make no attempt, then, to estimate the magnitude

U

of the gain or loss which the destruction of a belief in Providence and a future life would entail upon mankind. I merely endeavour to characterise one or two of the elements of which that gain or loss would be composed.

But in doing so I do not propose to count, or at least to consider, the feelings of satisfaction, or the reverse, with which, according to their temper or their creed, individuals may contemplate their personal destiny after death. My present business is with thoughts and emotions of a wider reference, and among these I count the effect which the belief that physical dissolution is not the destruction of consciousness, that death lets down the curtain at the end of the act not at the end of the piece, has upon the mood in which we survey the darker aspects of the world in which we live.

I. To say that the doctrine of Immortality provides us with a ready-made solution of the problem of evil, is of course absurd. If there be a problem, it is insoluble. Nevertheless there can be no doubt that it may profoundly modify the whole attitude of mind in which we are able to face the insistent facts of sin, suffering, and misery. I am no pessimist. I do not profess to weigh against one another the sorrows and the joys of humanity, and to conclude that it had been better for us had we never been born.   Let any one try to perform such a calculation in his own case (about which he may be presumed to have exceptional sources of information); let him, in the same spirit of unimpassioned inquiry in which he would carry on any other piece of scientific measurement, attempt to estimate how much of his life has been above and how much below that neutral line which represents the precise degree of wellbeing at which existence is neither a blessing nor a curse, and he will henceforth treat with derision all attempts to perform the same operation for the human race.

But though this be so, yet the sense of misery unrelieved, of wrongs unredressed, of griefs beyond remedy, of failure without hope, of physical pain so acute that it seems the one overmastering reality in a world of shadows, of mental depression so deadly that it welcomes physical pain itself as a relief— these, and all the crookednesses and injustices of a crooked and unjust world, may well overload our spirits and shatter the springs of our energies, if to this world only we must restrict our gaze.   For thus

narrowed the problem is hopeless.   Let us dream
what dreams we please about the future; let us paint
it in hues of our own choosing; let us fashion for
ourselves a world in which war has been abolished,
disease mitigated, poverty rooted out; in which
justice and charity determine every relation in life,
and we shall still leave untouched a residue of irremediable ills—separation, decay, weariness, death.
This distant and doubtful millennium has its dark
shadows: and then how distant and doubtful it is!
The most intrepid prophet dare hardly say with
assurance whether the gorgeous mountain shapes to
which we are drifting be cloud or solid earth.   And
while the future happiness is doubtful, the present
misery is certain.   Nothing that humanity can enjoy
in the future will make up for what it has suffered
in the past: for those who will enjoy are not the
same as those who have suffered: one set of persons
is injured, another set will receive compensation.

Now I do not wish to be guilty of any exaggeration.   It may freely be conceded that many persons
exist to whom the knowledge that there are wrongs
to be remedied is a stimulus to remedying them, and
is nothing more; who can abstract their minds from

everything but the work in hand, and remain, like an experienced doctor, wholly undisturbed by the sufferings of those whom they are endeavouring to relieve. But I am not sure that this class is common, or is getting commoner. The sensitiveness to social evils is increasing, and it is good that it should increase. But the good is not unmixed. In proportion as the general sympathy gets wider, as the social imagination gets more comprehensive and more responsive, so will the number of those increase who according to their temper either rush frantically to the first quack remedy that presents itself, or, too clear-sighted to be sanguine, but not callous enough to be indifferent, yield themselves bondsmen to a sceptical despair. For the first of these classes I know not that anything can be done. There is no cure for stupidity. But for the second, the faith that what we see is but part, and a small part, of a general scheme which will complete the destiny, not merely of humanity, but (which is a very different thing) of every man, woman, and child born into the world, has supplied, and may again supply, consolation and encouragement, energy and hope.

II. It is true that we are sometimes told that a

system by which rewards and punishments are annexed in another world, to the practice of virtue or of vice in this one, appeals to the baser side of human nature. And comparisons are drawn between religions which appeal to such sanctions, and religions which do not, entirely to the disadvantage of the former. But this opinion, which lends itself naturally to much easy rhetorical treatment, is open to more than one objection. In the first place, it mistakes the position which the doctrine of future retribution holds in Christian theology, a position which, though real and important, is nevertheless a subordinate one in the hierarchy of religious motives. On this I do not further dwell, since it obviously falls beyond the limit of my present subject. But in the second place, it seems altogether to mistake the true position of rational self-love in any sound scheme of practical morality.

Conceive for one moment what an infinitely better and happier world it would be if every action in it were directed by a reasonable desire for the agent's happiness ! Excess of all kinds, drunkenness and its attendant ills, would vanish ; disease would be enormously mitigated ; nine-tenths of the petty vexations which embitter domestic life would be smoothed away ; the competition for wealth would be lessened, for wealth would be rated at no more than the quantity of pleasure which it is capable of purchasing for its possessor; the sympathetic emotions would be sedulously cultivated, as among those least subject to weariness and satiety; while self-sacrifice itself would be practised as the last refinement of a judicious luxury.

Now, love of self thus understood, we should be right in ranking infinitely lower among springs of action than the love of God or the love of man. But we should assuredly be utterly wrong in confounding it with self-indulgence, of which it is usually the precise opposite, or in describing it as in any respect base and degraded. The world suffers not because it has too much of it, but because it has too little ; not because it displaces higher motives, but because it is itself habitually displaced by lower ones. But though this be so, yet it must sometimes happen, however rarely, that rational love of self conflicts with the disinterested love of man, if results in this world alone be taken into account. It is only if we are permitted to assume another phase of existence in

direct moral relation with this one, that the contra-
diction between these guiding principles of conduct
can be solved certainly and universally in a higher
harmony.

It is true that hopes are held out to us that a
judicious manipulation of the latent forces of public
opinion may supply us with a very efficient substitute
for Heaven and Hell, and may provide a method by
which any action disagreeable to the community shall
be made so intolerable to its perpetrator, that a perfect
accord will be produced between individual and public
interests. Now I am far indeed from asserting that
this scheme (which oddly enough meets with especial
favour from those who find something unworthy of
the highest morality in the ordinary doctrine of
future retribution) is wholly chimerical. The effect
which the opinion of his habitual associates has upon
the ordinary man, who is neither a hero nor a scoundrel,
is almost limitless: and though I do not know that
their approval has been able as yet to give its object
a foretaste of Heaven, their disapproval may, without
doubt, be so organised as to supply its victim with a
very sufficient anticipation of Hell. But is this a
power which any sober man desires to see indefinitely

increased and placed in irresponsible hands? Is there the slightest possibility that its operation would be limited to questions of morals? Would it not inevitably trespass upon individual freedom in neutral matters? Would it not crush out every germ of that "tendency to variation" which is the very basis of development? and can we seriously regard it as an improvement in the scheme of the universe that Infinite Justice and Infinite Mercy should be dethroned for the purpose of putting in their place an apotheosised Mrs. Grundy?

Dismissing, then, this substitute for future retribution as a remedy more dangerous than the disease, let us take stock of the position in which practical morality is left by the abolition of a future life. I have sketched for you what the world might be if it were governed solely by reasonable self-love; and a comparison between this picture and the reality should satisfy any one how feeble a motive self-love is compared with the work which it has to perform. In this lies the explanation of a fact which, strangely enough, has been used as an argument to show the worthlessness of Christianity as an instrument for moralising the world. How comes it, say these

objectors, that in the ages when (as they read history)
the sufferings and joys of eternity were present with
special vividness to the mind of Christendom, more
effect was not produced upon the lives of men; that
licentiousness and devotion so often went hand in
hand; that the terrors of Hell and the hopes of
Heaven were powerless to stay the hand of violence
and oppression? The answer is, that then, as now,
the conviction that happiness lies along one road and
misery along another, is seldom adequate to determine the path of the traveller. He will choose the
wrong way, knowing it to be the wrong way, and
well assured in his moments of reflection that he is
doing not merely what he knows to be wicked, but
what he knows to be inexpedient. Surely, however,
this is not only conformable to the facts of human
nature, but to the doctrines of Christianity. If the
practice of the noblest conduct is a fruit that can
spring from the enlightened desire for happiness,
then have theologians in all ages been notably mistaken. But it is not so. However closely in theory
the actions prescribed by self-love may agree with
those prescribed by benevolence, no man has ever
succeeded in performing them from the former motive

alone.   No conviction, for instance, that unselfishness "pays" has ever made any man habitually and successfully unselfish.   To promote the happiness of others solely as a means to our own, may be, and is, a perfectly logical and reasonable policy, but it is not a policy which human beings are capable of pursuing : and, as experience shows that the love of self must be barren unless merged in the love of others, so does the Church teach that rarely can this love of others be found in its highest perfection unless associated with the love of God.   These three great principles—great, but not co-equal, distinct in themselves, harmonious in the actions they prescribe, gaining strength from a combination often so intimate as to defy analysis, are yet, even in combination, insufficient to control the inordinate ambitions, desires, and passions over which they are *de jure*, but seldom *de facto*, the unquestioned rulers.   How, then, are they dealt with by the Positivist creed ?   The love of self is *directly* weakened as a motive to virtue by the abolition of supernatural sanctions in another life. The love of others is *indirectly* weakened by the possibility of conflict between it and the love of self. The love of God is summarily suppressed.   Surely those who can contemplate this result with equanimity must either be very indifferent to the triumph of morality, very ignorant of human nature, or very sanguine about the issues of the struggle between the opposing forces of good and evil.

III. In considering, however, the effect of any creed on human actions, it is a great though a common error to limit our view to the bare substance of the morality it advocates, or to the direct method by which moral action is to be produced. Scarcely less important is the manner in which it presents the results of human effort to the imagination of men. The question, Is life worth living? when it is not a mere exclamation of weariness and satiety, means or should mean, Is there any object worth striving for, not merely as a matter of duty, but for its intrinsic greatness? Can we look at the labours of man from any point of view which shall satisfy, not the conscience merely, but also the imagination? For if not, if the best we can say of life is that, though somewhat lacking in meaning, yet where circumstances are propitious, it is not otherwise than agreeable, then assuredly in our moments of reflection it would *not* seem worth living; and the more we contemplate it as a whole, the more we raise ourselves above the distractions of the passing moment, the less worth living will it seem.

This, I apprehend, would not be denied by any Positivist, but he would claim for his creed that it had an ideal object, vast enough to absorb the whole energies of mankind, and splendid enough to satisfy its highest aspirations. In the work of building up a perfected humanity, every one may bear a part. None indeed can do much, yet all may do something. During his brief journey from nothingness to nothingness, each man may add his pebble to the slowly-rising foundations of an ideal world, content to pass into eternal darkness if he has hastened by a moment the advent of the golden age which, though he will not live to see it, yet must surely come.

Though personally I prefer a system under which we may share the millennium to which we are invited to contribute, I should be the last to deny that conduct thus inspired has much in it that appeals to the highest imagination. But though the ideal is grand, is it also "positive"? I have never been able to discover that there is any foundation in the known laws of nature for these flattering anticipations, or for any confident expectation that if perfection be attainable we are in the right way to attain it. Consider for a moment the complexity of human affairs : our ignorance of the laws which govern the growth of societies; the utter inadequacy of any power of calculation that we possess to apply with confidence our knowledge of those laws (such as it is) to the guidance of the contending forces by which the social organisation is moved. The man who would sacrifice the good of the next generation for the greater good of the generation next but one is a fool. He neglects an age of which he may know a little, for the sake of an age respecting which he can know nothing. He might, if he pleased, stumble along in the twilight; he prefers to adventure himself in the blackness of utter night. Yet what is a generation in the history of man? Nothing. And we, who cannot be sure whether our efforts will benefit or injure our grandchildren, are quietly to assume that we are in the way to contribute to the fortunes of the remotest representatives of the human race.

It will perhaps be said that if we do our best, all these things shall be added unto us; and that, without conscious contrivance on our part we shall be gently led towards the final consummation by that modern Providence the principle of Evolution. But I have never been fortunate enough to persuade myself that evolution, in so far as it is a scientific doctrine, promises all or any of these good things. I am aware that occasionally evolutionists also find themselves among the prophets; and I take it that some of these anticipations are conceived in the spirit of prophecy rather than in that of natural philosophy. But what guidance in this matter is actually given us by science? We are taught that the successive developments of species have not been along one main channel, but in countless branching streams, like those that intersect the delta of some great river. We also know that at some point or other on the way towards the development of a higher intelligence all these streams but one have been checked. The progenitors of man, and they alone, would seem to have hit off the precise line of flow, which could produce an Aristotle or a Newton. But because man, more fortunate than his cousins, has got thus far, is his future progress to be indefinite? If he differs from the animals only in degree, will not his fate only differ from theirs in degree also? He too will reach a point, if he has not reached it already, beyond which no variation will bring with it increased intellectual grasp, increased vigour of imagination, increased moralisation of will, increased capacity for social life. Nor does it seem to me that the study of history leads us to more encouraging results. There, too, progress has not been along one line of descent. Races and nations have in turn taken up the burden of advancing civilisation, borne it for a certain space, found it too heavy for them, and have laid it wearily down. Many peoples have degenerated, many have become stationary, and I am wholly at a loss to know why we—the group of Western nations—and we alone, may hope to escape the common destiny of man.

If we, then, regard the Universe in which we have to live as a mere web of connected phenomena, created for no object, informed by no purpose, stamped with no marks of design other than those which can be imitated by Natural Selection, I see no ground for the faith that all honest effort will work together for the production of a regenerate man and a perfected society. Such a conclusion cannot be drawn from the notion of God, for by hypothesis there is no God. It cannot be drawn from any

general survey of the plan on which the world is
framed, or of the end for which it is constructed :
for the world is framed on no plan, nor is it constructed to carry out any end. It cannot be drawn
from a consideration of the histories of individual
species or nations, for the inference to be drawn
from these is that Nature has set bounds beyond
which no alteration brings with it any sensible
improvement. It cannot be deduced from what we
know of man, for we have no knowledge of man more
certain than that he is powerless consciously to bend
towards the attainment of any remote ideal, forces
whose interaction he is powerless to calculate or to
comprehend. To me, therefore, it seems that the
"positive" view of the world must needs end in a
chilling scepticism concerning the final worth of
human effort, which can hardly fail to freeze and
paralyse the warmest enthusiasm and the most
zealous energy.

IV. But I do not think that its effects in starving
what I may perhaps be allowed to call the "moral
imagination" end here. There are some who hold
that the wider range of vision given to us by history
and science has diminished the credibility of a religion

X

which comparative theology tells us is only one among thousands that have flourished on a planet of which astronomy tells us that it is only one among indefinite millions scattered through limitless space. For my own part, the conclusion I draw from these undoubted facts is precisely the opposite one. Comte was, I think, well advised when, in his later writings, he discouraged research into matters remote from obvious human interest, on the ground that such research is inimical to the progress of the Positive faith. Not Christianity, but Positivism, shrinks and pales in the light of increasing knowledge. For, while the Positive faith professes to base itself upon science, its emotions centre in humanity, and we are therefore treated to the singular spectacle of a religion in which each great advance in the doctrines which support it dwarfs still further the dignity of the object for which it exists. For what is man, considered merely as a natural object among other natural objects? Time was when the fortunes of his tribe were enough to exhaust the energies and to bound the imagination of the primitive sage. The gods' peculiar care, the central object of an attendant universe, that for which the sun shone and the dew fell, to which the stars in their courses ministered; it drew its origin in the past from divine ancestors, and might by divine favour be destined to an indefinite existence of success and triumph in the future.

These ideas represent no early stage in human thought, but we have left them far behind. The family, the tribe, the nation, are no longer enough to absorb our interests. Man, past, present, and future, lays claim to our devotion. What, then, can we say of him?

Man, so far as natural science by itself is able to teach us, is no longer the final cause of the universe, the heaven-descended heir of all the ages. His very existence is an accident, his story a brief and discreditable episode in the life of one of the meanest of the planets. Of the combination of causes which first converted a piece or pieces of unorganised jelly into the living progenitors of humanity, science indeed, as yet, knows nothing. It is enough that from such beginnings Famine, Disease, and Mutual Slaughter, fit nurses of the future lord of creation, have gradually evolved, after infinite travail, a race with conscience enough to know that it is vile, and intelligence enough to know that it is insignificant.

We survey the past and see that its history is of blood and tears, of helpless blundering, of wild revolt, of stupid acquiescence, of empty aspirations. We sound the future, and learn that after a period, long compared with the individual life, but short indeed compared with the divisions of time open to our investigation, the energies of our system will decay, the glory of the sun will be dimmed, and the earth, tideless and inert, will no longer tolerate the race which has for a moment disturbed its solitude. Man will go down into the pit, and all his thoughts will perish. The uneasy consciousness, which in this obscure corner has for a brief space broken the contented silence of the Universe, will be at rest. Matter will know itself no longer. Imperishable monuments and immortal deeds, death itself, and love stronger than death, will be as though they had never been. Nor will anything that remains be better or be worse for all that the labour, genius, devotion, and suffering of man have striven through countless generations to effect.

Now this Positivist eschatology, like any other eschatology, need of course have little obvious or direct bearing on the great mass of ordinary everyday interests and emotions.   It need not overshadow every thought and action of him who accepts it, any more than the knowledge that death must come some time, and may come soon, thrusts itself obtrusively into the business and enjoyment of the average man. But this does not mean that its influence can be disregarded.   One of the objects of the "religion of humanity," and it is an object beyond all praise, is to stimulate the imagination till it lovingly embraces the remotest fortunes of the whole human family. But in proportion as this end is successfully attained, in proportion as we are taught by this or any other religion to neglect the transient and the personal, and to count ourselves as labourers for that which is universal and abiding, so surely must the increasing range which science is giving to our vision over the times and spaces of the material universe, and the decreasing importance of the place which man is seen to occupy in it, strike coldly on our moral imagination, if so be that the material universe is all we have to do with.   It is no answer to say that scientific discovery cannot alter the moral law, and that so long as the moral law is unchanged our conduct need be modified by no opinions as to the future destiny of this planet or its inhabitants. This contention, whether true or not, is irrelevant. All developed religions, and all philosophies which aspire to take the place of religion, Lucretius as well as St. Paul, give us some theory as to the destiny of man and his relation to the sum of things. My contention is that every such religion and every such philosophy, so long as it insists on regarding man as merely a phenomenon among phenomena, a natural object among other natural objects, is condemned by science to failure as an effective stimulus to high endeavour. Love, pity, and endurance it may indeed leave with us: and this is well. But it so dwarfs and impoverishes the ideal end of human effort, that though it may encourage us to die with dignity, it hardly permits us to live with hope.

I have now endeavoured briefly to indicate certain salient points in which, as I think, Positivism must, even within the limits of mundane experience, prove inferior as a moralising agent to Christianity. Of the inmost essence of Christianity, of the doctrines dealing with the personal relations between God and man, in which it differs not merely from Positivism, but from all other forms of religion, I have said little.

For Positivism, not Christianity, is my subject, and
over this region of religious consciousness Positivism
claims no sway. I have contented myself with
inquiring which of these two is in truth the better
"religion of humanity"; which is the religion most
fitted, in the face of advancing knowledge, to con-
centrate in the service of man those high emotions
and far-reaching hopes from which the moral law,
as a practical system, draws nourishment and strength.
That such a method of treatment is essentially incom-
plete is of course obvious. It arbitrarily isolates, and
exclusively deals with, but a small fraction of the question at issue between supernaturalism and naturalism.
It leaves out of account the greatest question of
all—namely, the question of comparative proof, and
directs attention only to the less august problem of
comparative advantage. Such a limitation of treatment would in any case be imposed by the character
of the occasion, but I am not sure that it is not in-
trinsically useful. A philosophy of belief, I do not
mean of religious belief, exclusively or even principally, but of all belief, has yet to be constructed. I
do not know that its foundations are yet laid; nor
are they likely to be laid by Positivist thinkers, on

whose minds it does not for the most part seem yet
to have dawned that such a philosophy is in any way
required.   Until some progress is made in this work
I must adhere to an opinion which I have elsewhere
defended, that much current controversy about the
possibility of miracles, about the evidence for design,
about what is commonly, though very absurdly,
described as the "conflict between science and
religion," can at best be only provisional.   But when
the time comes at which mankind shall have attained
some coherent method of testing the validity of those
opinions respecting the natural and the spiritual
worlds on which in their best moments they desire
to act, then I hazard the guess, since to guesses we
are at present confined, that adaptation to the moral
wants and aspirations of humanity will not be regarded as wholly alien to the problems over which
so many earnest minds are at present disquieting
themselves in vain.

But even apart from the question of relative proof,
it may be said that the comparison between Christianity and Positivism has been very incompletely
worked out.   This is true, but let it be noted that
the incompleteness of treatment is unfavourable, not

to Positivism, but to Christianity. We have compared Positivism where it is thought to be strongest, with Christianity where it is thought to be weakest. And if the result of the comparison even there has been unfavourable to Positivism, how will the account stand if every element in Christianity be taken into consideration? The "religion of humanity" seems specially fitted to meet the tastes of that comparatively small and prosperous class, who are unwilling to leave the dry bones of Agnosticism wholly unclothed with any living tissue of religious emotion, and who are at the same time fortunate enough to be able to persuade themselves that they are contributing, or may contribute, by their individual efforts to the attainment of some great ideal for mankind. But what has it to say to the more obscure multitude who are absorbed, and wellnigh overwhelmed, in the constant struggle with daily needs and narrow cares; who have but little leisure or inclination to consider the precise *rôle* they are called on to play in the great drama of "humanity," and who might in any case be puzzled to discover its interest or its importance? Can it assure them that there is no human being so insignificant as not to be of infinite worth in the eyes of Him who created the Heavens, or so feeble but that his action may have consequence of infinite moment long after this material system shall have crumbled into nothingness? Does it offer consolation to those who are in grief, hope to those who are bereaved, strength to the weak, forgiveness to the sinful, rest to those who are weary and heavy laden? If not, then, whatever be its merits, it is no rival to Christianity. It cannot penetrate and vivify the inmost life of ordinary humanity. There is in it no nourishment for ordinary human souls, no comfort for ordinary human sorrow, no help for ordinary human weakness. Not less than the crudest irreligion does it leave us men divorced from all communion with God, face to face with the unthinking energies of nature which gave us birth, and into which, if supernatural religion be indeed a dream, we must after a few fruitless struggles be again resolved.

THE END